CONFESSIONS OF POWER

NIRBHAY VASSA

notionpress.com

INDIA · SINGAPORE · MALAYSIA

ISBN
Paperback 979-8-89498-804-7
Hardcase 979-8-89556-336-6

I miss you papa.
This one is for you.

Why Read This Book

This book is not just a guide to effective leadership; it is a roadmap to personal and professional growth. It offers insights, strategies, and real-world examples to help you navigate the complexities of leadership and develop the skills needed to succeed. Whether you are an aspiring leader or an experienced one, this book provides valuable lessons that will inspire and empower you to lead with empathy, integrity, and resilience.

***

Nirbhay's story is one of hope and determination, a shining example of how one can turn challenges into opportunities and dreams into reality. His insights and experiences are a beacon for anyone striving to navigate the complexities of leadership in today's world.

It is with great pride and admiration that I introduce *Confessions of Power*. May this book inspire you as much as Nirbhay has inspired all those who have had the fortune to know him.

Abhishek Bansal, Founder and Chairman
–Abans Holdings Ltd

Nirbhay's ability to nurture & develop more leaders is his best quality of a leader. Not only that - he also has an innate ability to hook & engage an audience in a manner that he may not be aware himself. But I've seen it leaving lasting impressions on all around him.

I'm positive all of us can find this mindset inculcation in "Confessions of Power" & use it to charge through life with more deliberation.

Pratham Barot, CEO & Founder
–Zell Education

Acknowledgments

- To my dearest family, who are the bedrock of my life and the foundation of all my endeavors. To Misha, my loving wife, whose unwavering support and love have been my guiding light. To Bhavna, my beloved mother, whose wisdom and care have shaped me into who I am today. And to Dhairya, my wonderful brother, whose camaraderie and strength have always been a source of inspiration.
- To my in-laws, who have always believed in me and manifested my success.
- To my friends, each one an influence and a cherished part of my journey. Your laughter, counsel, and presence have enriched my life in countless ways.
- To my colleagues, with whom I have shared both challenges and triumphs. Your dedication and teamwork have made every goal achievable and every day rewarding.
- To my mentors, whose guidance has been invaluable; and to my mentees, whose trust and growth have been a joy to witness.
- To my gurus, who have imparted knowledge and wisdom; and to my students, who have inspired me with their curiosity and passion.
- To Gauri Shrotri, who has sketched the cover page herself. Her remarkable turnaround times and zest for my book have been

so exciting and deeply appreciated. The idea and the outcome are entirely credited to you, Gauri. I am deeply indebted to you for your hard work and creativity. I believe in your potential and see you going a long way in your career. Thank you for being such a crucial part of this journey.

- To all the people who have touched my life and inspired me along the way—this book has only been possible because of how you have touched my life. Each of you holds a special place in my heart, and I am eternally grateful for the role you have played in my story.

With heartfelt gratitude,

–Nirbhay

Index

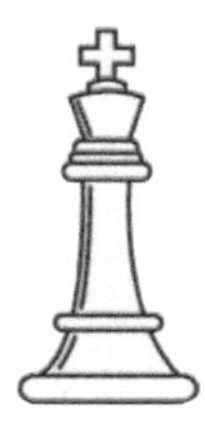

Words of a Mentor

When I first met Nirbhay Vassa, I was deeply moved by how his strength was always paired with such genuine compassion. Here was someone who had faced formidable challenges early in life, but had emerged not only stronger but also profoundly empathetic and insightful. Over the years, as I got to know him better, I saw firsthand the qualities that make him an extraordinary leader and mentor.

As Nirbhay's mentor, I have had the privilege of witnessing his remarkable journey up close. His transformation from a determined young professional into a distinguished, Certified Chartered Accountant, and Executive Director of our company has been nothing short of inspiring.

Nirbhay's professional acumen is unparalleled, but it's his ability to connect with people that truly sets him apart. He has a rare talent for understanding the struggles of those around him and inspiring them to achieve their best. Whether navigating complex financial landscapes or mentoring aspiring professionals, Nirbhay's leadership is characterised by integrity, empathy, and unwavering commitment.

Confessions of Power is more than a memoir; it's a guide to leading with heart and mind. Through personal anecdotes, powerful reflections, and the wisdom gleaned from mentors and mentees alike, Nirbhay offers a candid look into the essence of true leadership. His journey is filled with moments of introspection, stories of overcoming adversity, and lessons that resonate with anyone seeking to make a meaningful impact.

I have seen Nirbhay tackle challenges with grace and determination, always striving to lift others as he climbs. His leadership is not about commanding authority, but about earning respect through consistent acts of kindness and understanding. This book encapsulates his spirit, offering valuable insights for both new and seasoned professionals.

Reading *Confessions of Power*, you will not only learn about the principles that have guided Nirbhay's journey, but also be inspired to reflect on your own path. You will find yourself encouraged to embrace your vulnerabilities, build meaningful connections, and lead with both head and heart.

Nirbhay's story is one of hope and determination, a shining example of how one can turn challenges into opportunities and dreams into reality. His insights and experiences are a beacon for anyone striving to navigate the complexities of leadership in today's world.

It is with great pride and admiration that I introduce *Confessions of Power*. May this book inspire you as much as Nirbhay has inspired all those who have had the fortune to know him.

—Abhishek Bansal

The Journey Begins

In the quiet moments between balancing ledgers and reviewing financial reports, I often find myself lost in the beauty of a well-crafted quote or the elegance of a poem. Leadership, much like poetry, is an art form – a delicate balance between the structured and the emotional, the rational and the intuitive. My journey as a chartered accountant has taken me through various leadership roles, each one teaching me invaluable lessons about the human side of power and influence.

This book, *Confessions of Power*, is a culmination of those lessons, shaped by my experiences and the many individuals who have walked alongside me. It's a story about finding the harmony between professional rigour and personal passion, about the romance of leading with both heart and mind.

I remember the first time I felt the weight of leadership. I was young, ambitious, and eager to prove myself. But beneath that determination, there was a heart full of doubt and a mind constantly questioning if I was good enough. Over time, I learned that true leadership isn't about having all the answers, but about embracing the journey and learning from every step.

My mother, with her determination and gentle wisdom, was my first mentor. Growing up in a small town in Gujarat, she dreamed of a better life for me and worked tirelessly to help me fit into the bustling culture of Mumbai. Her strength became my inspiration, and her words of encouragement, my guiding light.

As I navigated my professional path, moving to London presented new challenges. My accent and cultural background made me feel out of place, but it also taught me the importance of resilience and adaptability. Slowly, I found my footing, and, with it, a renewed confidence that allowed me to lead with authenticity.

Leadership also brought me close to remarkable mentors like Suresh and Abhishek. Suresh taught me the essence of unwavering commitment, while Abhishek pushed me to explore my full potential. Their guidance was instrumental in shaping my leadership style, one that balances empathy with ambition.

Throughout my career, I've had the privilege of mentoring others. These interactions, often more rewarding than any professional achievement, reminded me of the power of human connection. It's in these moments, sharing wisdom, and watching others grow, that I truly understood the impact of leadership.

In *Confessions of Power*, you'll find not just my stories, but also the poetry and quotes that have inspired me along the way. From the resilience of M.S. Dhoni to the strategic brilliance of leaders like Nelson Mandela, the pages of this book are homage to the many facets of leadership.

This is not a conventional leadership manual. It's a heartfelt exploration of what it means to lead with grace, humility, and passion. Whether you're a seasoned leader or just starting on your journey, I hope my confessions offer you insights and inspiration.

To my readers, I invite you to walk this path with me. Embrace the poetry in your leadership, find strength in your vulnerabilities, and remember that true power comes from leading with your heart.

As Batman once said, "It's not who I am underneath, but what I do that defines me." *Welcome to Confessions of Power.* This is my story, and these are my confessions.

The Heartbeat Behind My Words: Why I Write Poetry

Life is a tapestry of experiences, woven together by the threads of our thoughts, actions, and emotions. As I reflect on my journey—both personal and professional—I've come to realize that leadership is not just about guiding others; it's about understanding oneself, embracing vulnerability, and finding strength in the connections we make along the way.

For me, poetry has always been a refuge—a place where I can explore the depths of my emotions and express the unspoken truths that lie within. Poetry has shaped my worldview, influencing how I lead, how I connect with others, and how I navigate the challenges that life presents. Throughout this book, you will find glimpses of this poetic influence, woven into the narrative as a reflection of the lessons I've learned and the emotions I've experienced.

Poetic Reflection

In words, I find a place to rest,
Where thoughts take flight and hearts confess.
In verses brief, yet deeply felt,
The stories of our lives are dealt.

Through poetry, I've learned to see,
The truths that often hide from me.
In every line, a lesson lies,
In every rhyme, a path to rise

Chapter One

The Many Faces of Leadership

Leadership is a word that often brings to mind images of CEOs in boardrooms, politicians at podiums, or generals in the field. However, the essence of leadership extends far beyond these stereotypes. It's present in our daily lives, often in the most unexpected places. It's in the decisions we make, the relationships we build, and the challenges we face. Leadership is a subtle yet powerful force shaping our world.

Leadership in Everyday Life

Imagine a single mother, juggling multiple jobs to provide for her children. She's not just keeping the household running; she's setting an example of resilience and determination. She leads by showing her kids that no matter how tough life gets, you push through. Her leadership isn't recognised with titles or awards, but it's impactful, nonetheless.

In schools, leadership can be seen in the student who steps up to help a classmate struggling with their homework, or the one who organises a group project, ensuring everyone contributes and learns. These young leaders might not hold official positions, but they are making a difference in their own quiet ways.

Among friends, leadership often shows up in the person who plans the gatherings, resolves conflicts, or simply listens when others need to talk. This kind of leadership builds trust and strengthens bonds, creating a support network that is vital for personal growth and well-being.

My Journey: An Ordinary Boy's Tale

My journey into leadership started in a rather humble way. Born into a wealthy family, I had access to opportunities that many could only dream of. My mother, a strong-willed woman from a small town in Gujarat, worked tirelessly to ensure I fit into the vibrant, often overwhelming culture of Mumbai. She instilled in me the values of perseverance and resilience. However, life took a sharp turn when I was thirteen. We went broke, and my father's words—"We don't have anything, and you have to make it on your own"—echoed in my mind. It was a moment of truth that shaped my resolve.

Imagine a young boy, once sheltered by wealth, suddenly thrust into a world of uncertainty. The security I had known vanished overnight. Yet, it was in this crucible of hardship that I discovered the true essence of leadership. It wasn't about commanding others, but about finding strength within and guiding myself through the darkness.

Discovering Leadership in Unlikely Places

Always dreaming of becoming an automobile engineer, I was unable to fulfil that ambition due to a lack of resources. However, I managed to secure a visa to study in London, a city I had never been to before. The prospect of being alone for the first time in my life was terrifying. That solo flight to London was a pivotal moment that changed my life forever.

That flight to London was more than just a journey across continents; it was a journey into self-discovery. The fear and uncertainty of being alone in a foreign land forced me to dig deep and find strength I didn't know I had. The challenges I faced and the people I met along the way taught me that leadership is about more than just holding a position of authority. It's about resilience, adaptability, and the ability to inspire and connect with others.

Upon arriving in London, I faced a whirlwind of challenges. I quickly realised I had less than a month's worth of resources to survive. Desperate and determined, I applied for 25 jobs in my second week. It was during these trying times that I discovered leadership in the most unexpected places, and each experience became a source of inspiration.

Starting a new life in London as a young adult, I faced another set of challenges. My Indian accent and cultural differences initially made me feel out of place. But these experiences taught me resilience and adaptability. It took years of practice and countless moments of self-doubt to regain my confidence and establish myself as a leader in this new environment. I learned that leadership is not about being in control, but about connecting with people on a deeper level.

During this time, I took on various odd jobs to support myself and gain new experiences. Working as a salesman and retail cashier, I learned valuable lessons about leadership from these seemingly humble roles.

As a salesman, I discovered the importance of understanding customer needs, building relationships, and effectively communicating the value of a product. It wasn't just about making sales, but about connecting with people and earning their trust. Each interaction taught me patience, empathy, and the art of persuasion—skills that are crucial for any leader.

Working as a retail cashier, I experienced firsthand the significance of teamwork and efficiency. The job required me to manage time effectively, handle stressful situations with grace, and maintain a positive attitude even during long, tiring shifts. These experiences reinforced the value of hard work, dedication, and a customer-centric approach—principles that I carried into my leadership roles.

Each job, each interaction, and each moment of self-doubt became a brushstroke in the larger portrait of my life. I found inspiration in the everyday tasks and the people who crossed my path. From the customers I served to the colleagues I collaborated with, every experience enriched my understanding of leadership. I learned that leadership qualities can be developed in any situation, no matter how humble or challenging it may seem.

Through these seemingly ordinary jobs, I found leadership in the most unexpected places. The lessons learned during this time shaped my approach to leading others with empathy, patience, and a genuine connection. My journey in London taught me that true leadership is about inspiring others, cultivating responsibility, and leading with integrity. It's about finding strength in adversity, and turning every challenge into an opportunity for growth.

The Magic of Leadership

Leadership often means rising to the occasion, even when you don't feel ready. It's about making decisions in the face of uncertainty and guiding others through the unknown. Take Mahendra Singh

Dhoni, for example. The former captain of the Indian cricket team is renowned for his calm demeanour and strategic acumen. Dhoni led India to numerous victories, not just through his cricketing skills, but through his ability to inspire and unify his team under pressure.

Dhoni's leadership style is a perfect blend of resilience and calmness. During the 2007 ICC World Twenty20 final, when India was on the brink of victory or defeat, Dhoni made a daring decision to give the final over to Joginder Sharma, a relatively inexperienced bowler. This unexpected move paid off, and India won the tournament. Dhoni's belief in his team, and his ability to stay composed under immense pressure, exemplify the essence of true leadership.

Leadership also emerges in grassroots movements. Think of the young activists fighting for climate change or social justice. Their leadership isn't driven by titles or positions, but by passion and a vision for a better world. Greta Thunberg, for instance, started her climate activism alone, skipping school to protest outside the Swedish parliament. Her solitary protest sparked a global movement, "Fridays for Future," inspiring millions of students worldwide to demand action on climate change. Thunberg's leadership is a testament to how a single individual's conviction can galvanise a global response.

Consider Malala Yousafzai, who stood up for girls' education in Pakistan. Despite being attacked by the Taliban, Malala's resolve only grew stronger. She co-authored the memoir "I Am Malala" and became the youngest-ever Nobel Prize laureate. Her courage and unwavering dedication to education have made her an international symbol of the fight for girls' rights and education, proving that leadership can arise from the most challenging circumstances.

Leadership manifests in diverse settings beyond the public eye. In the corporate world, Satya Nadella's transformation of Microsoft is noteworthy. When Nadella became CEO in 2014, he shifted the company's culture from a rigid, competitive environment to one that values empathy, continuous learning, and collaboration. His leadership rejuvenated Microsoft, driving significant growth and innovation. Nadella's approach highlights that effective leadership often involves fostering a positive and inclusive culture.

In everyday life, leadership can be seen in teachers who go beyond the curriculum to inspire their students. Consider Erin Gruwell, an American teacher whose story was depicted in the movie "Freedom Writers". Gruwell worked with at-risk students in a high school plagued by violence and racial tensions. Through her innovative teaching methods and unwavering belief in her students, she transformed their lives and helped them find their voices through writing. Gruwell's story demonstrates how leadership in education can change lives and build futures.

Leadership also exists in unexpected places. During the 2011 Fukushima nuclear disaster in Japan, a group of elderly volunteers, known as the "Skilled Veterans Corps," offered to replace younger workers in the hazardous clean-up efforts. Their selfless act of courage and responsibility not only protected the younger generation, but also exemplified leadership driven by wisdom and sacrifice.

In sports, grassroots movements, corporate environments, classrooms, and even in disaster-stricken areas, leadership takes many forms. It is not confined to titles or positions but is defined by actions, decisions, and the ability to inspire others. Whether it's the calm and strategic leadership of Dhoni, the passionate activism of Thunberg, the courageous advocacy of Malala, the transformative vision of Nadella, the inspirational teaching of Gruwell, or the selfless bravery of the Skilled Veterans Corps, leadership is a dynamic and multifaceted force that can emerge from anyone, anywhere.

The Power of Friendships in Leadership

Leadership is a journey deeply intertwined with the relationships we build along the way. Among these, friendships hold a special place, providing us with a unique blend of support, wisdom, and honest feedback. Genuine friends are the ones who see us at our best and our worst, who challenge us to grow, and who stand by us through thick and thin. These friendships are not just a source of comfort; they form a crucial foundation for effective leadership. Each friend imparts lessons that become part of our leadership DNA, helping us navigate the complexities of life and leadership with greater wisdom and resilience.

Misha: The Steady Anchor

Misha, my wife, has been the steady anchor in my life—a role that transcends the boundaries of marriage and delves into the realm of true friendship. Our relationship, built on years of shared experiences, is a clear demonstration of the profound impact that a supportive partner can have on one's leadership journey. Misha embodies the qualities of resilience, patience, and unwavering support—qualities that have deeply influenced the way I lead.

From the very beginning, Misha has been there, witnessing every stage of my journey—from the ambitious dreams of my youth to the complex realities of adulthood. She has seen me at my most vulnerable, during times of doubt and fear, and at my strongest, when I've reached new heights of success. In every situation, Misha has been a calming presence, helping me stay grounded and focused. Her ability to provide a safe space for me to express my fears and vulnerabilities has been invaluable. She listens without judgment, offering insights that come from a place of deep understanding and love.

Misha's resilience is one of the most significant lessons she has imparted to me. No matter how turbulent the circumstances, she remains constant, helping me navigate through life's challenges with grace. She is the parachute that ensures I land safely when I'm overwhelmed by fears, bringing me back to reality and reminding me of what truly matters. Conversely, when I'm riding the highs of success, she keeps me grounded, ensuring that I don't lose sight of humility and balance. Her patience has taught me the importance of staying calm under pressure, a crucial trait for any leader.

Her ability to see through my facades and speak to my true self has kept me aligned with my values, reminding me that true leadership begins with self-awareness. Misha's influence has made me not only a better leader but also a better person. She has shown me that leadership is not just about guiding others but also about being anchored in your own values and staying true to your principles.

In this complex journey of life and leadership, Misha is the steady thread that weaves strength, depth, and resilience. As Ralph Waldo Emerson once said, "The only way to have a friend is to be one." Misha exemplifies this truth, teaching me that true partnership is about enduring support, understanding, and mutual respect. Her friendship is a living example of the power of love and the critical role it plays in shaping our leadership journey. I am eternally grateful for her presence in my life, for she has been, and continues to be, the foundation upon which I build my life and leadership.

Viraj: The Reflective Wisdom

Viraj, my childhood friend, has been more than just a companion—he has been the mirror I need in my life, reflecting both my strengths and weaknesses with unfiltered honesty. His presence has been a constant source of strength and clarity, especially during the most challenging times of my career. Viraj embodies the leadership quality of reflective wisdom, a trait that has been instrumental in my growth as a leader.

From our early days together, Viraj has always been the one to offer a listening ear and honest advice. He is the kind of friend who isn't afraid to tell me the truth, even when it's hard to hear. This ability to provide candid feedback without sugarcoating reality has been crucial in helping me see situations more clearly and make better decisions. Viraj's role in my life transcends the typical boundaries of friendship—he is my confidant, my critic, and my cheerleader, all rolled into one.

Whenever I've faced a tough decision or found myself at a crossroads, Viraj has been the person I turn to. He listens patiently as I talk through my dilemmas, never interrupting but always absorbing every word. His ability to offer honest, unfiltered perspectives is one of his greatest strengths. There was a particular incident during a critical phase of my career that highlighted Viraj's unique ability to provide perspective. I was grappling with a major decision that had significant implications for my team and my future. My emotions were running high, and I was struggling to see the situation objectively. I called Viraj, hoping for some clarity.

We met at our favorite coffee shop, a place that had witnessed many of our deep conversations over the years. As I laid out the details of my predicament, Viraj listened intently. When I finished, he paused for a moment before speaking. "You're looking at this from a very narrow angle," he began. "Have you considered how this might impact the team in the long run, not just in the immediate future?" His question forced me to step back and reevaluate my perspective. Viraj has a knack for identifying the broader implications of a situation, something I often miss when I'm too close to the problem.

One of the most valuable lessons Viraj has imparted is the importance of trusting others. His advice to delegate more and empower my team has led to better outcomes and has helped me become a more effective leader. His ability to balance honesty with empathy, delivering tough truths in a way that pushes me to grow rather than retreat, is what makes his advice so impactful.

Having Viraj in my life is like having a compass that always points me in the right direction. His unwavering support and candid feedback have been crucial in helping me navigate the complexities of leadership. He is the mirror that reflects not just my strengths but also the areas where I need to grow. In the grand tapestry of my life, Viraj's friendship is a thread that runs through every significant moment, adding depth and richness to my journey. His influence has been a steady reminder that true friends don't just comfort us—they challenge us to be better, to see more clearly, and to lead with greater wisdom and compassion.

Paras: The Beacon of Belief

Paras, a friend who has known me since childhood, has been a beacon of steadfast belief in my abilities, especially during times when I've doubted myself the most. His support has been instrumental in restoring my confidence during challenging periods of my career. Paras embodies the leadership quality of unshakeable faith—a trait that has been crucial in helping me push through moments of self-doubt and uncertainty.

There was a time in my career when I felt like I was teetering on the edge, plagued with constant self-doubt. Every decision I made felt like a potential misstep, and I began questioning my abilities, my judgment, and even my worth as a leader. The pressure was immense, and the fear of failure loomed over me like a dark cloud. It was during this turbulent period that Paras stepped in, offering support that went far beyond mere comforting words.

Paras has the rare ability to see beyond the surface, to recognize the strength and potential that I had temporarily lost sight of. His belief in me was unfaltering. He took the time to sit with me, to listen to my fears and doubts without judgment, reminding me of the resilience I had shown in the face of adversity in the past. His words were not just reassuring—they were a reflection of the person he knew me to be.

One evening, after a particularly grueling day, Paras and I sat down for a long conversation. I poured out my frustrations, fears, and deep-seated insecurities, confessing that I felt like I was failing and couldn't see a way forward. Paras listened patiently, letting me vent all the pent-up anxiety that had been weighing me down. When I had finally exhausted my words, Paras looked at me with a steady gaze and said, "You are stronger than you realize. You have faced tougher situations and come out stronger every time. This is just another challenge, and I have no doubt you will overcome it."

His words rekindled a spark of confidence within me. Paras reminded me of my core values—the principles that had guided me through my career. He spoke of my commitment to integrity, my dedication to my team, and my ability to inspire and lead with empathy. His belief in me helped me to see the challenges not as insurmountable obstacles, but as opportunities for growth and learning. With Paras's encouragement, I started to regain my footing, approaching my responsibilities with renewed determination and clarity. The fog of self-doubt began to lift, and I could once again see the path ahead.

Paras's consistent belief in me was a guiding light in the storm, leading me back to my strengths and capabilities. His support during that tough phase in my career taught me an invaluable lesson about the power of belief and encouragement. It reinforced the importance of having a strong support system and the impact that genuine, heartfelt support can have on a person's confidence and resilience. Thanks to Paras, I emerged from that period stronger, more self-assured, and ready to face new challenges with a renewed sense of purpose.

The Role of Friendships in Leadership

These friendships have been more than just personal connections—they have been vital to my development as a leader. Each friend has taught me different qualities—resilience, reflective wisdom, and steadfast belief—that I carry with me in my leadership journey. They have provided me with the strength, clarity, and encouragement needed to navigate the complexities of leadership.

In leadership, having friends who are honest and supportive is essential. These friendships prevent us from becoming isolated in our decision-making processes and ensure that we remain open to feedback. They remind us of our humanity, teaching us that leadership is not just about achieving goals but about building meaningful relationships along the way.

In summary, the power of friendships in leadership cannot be overstated. Friends who offer honest feedback and steadfast support play a pivotal role in our growth and success. They help us navigate challenges, celebrate our victories, and, most importantly, remind us of our true potential. As we journey through the complexities of leadership, it is these friendships that provide the strength, clarity, and encouragement we need to lead with confidence and authenticity.

The Influence of Mentorship

Mentorship is another cornerstone of effective leadership. Throughout my journey, I have been fortunate to have mentors who guided me with their wisdom and experience. Suresh, whom I met in London, taught me the true meaning of commitment. His dedication to his work and unwavering principles were a source of inspiration. Abhishek, my current boss, pushed me to realise my full potential. His belief in my abilities helped me see beyond my self-imposed limitations.

Mentorship is not just about receiving guidance; it's about developing a relationship based on mutual respect and trust. It involves honest feedback, encouragement, and sometimes, tough love. My mentors didn't just tell me what I wanted to hear; they challenged me, pushed me out of my comfort zone, and helped me grow. We will visit mentorship in more detail in this book.

Interactive Reflection

Let's take a moment to reflect on your own experiences. Have you ever stepped up in a difficult situation? Have you taken on responsibilities that were not part of your job description because you saw a need? These are all acts of leadership. Leadership is not about titles or positions; it's about action and influence.

- What does leadership mean to you?
- Think about moments when you felt compelled to lead. What drove you?
- Can you recall a time when someone's leadership had a significant impact on your life? What did they do, and how did it affect you?

Thought-Provoking Insights

Leadership is a journey of continuous learning and growth. It requires self-awareness, empathy, and a willingness to take risks. Here are some questions to ponder:

- How do you handle failure? Leaders often face setbacks. What matters is how you respond to them.
- What qualities do you admire in leaders? Reflecting on these qualities can help you cultivate them in yourself.
- How can you inspire others? Leadership is about influence. How can you positively impact those around you?

Leadership is a multifaceted concept that touches every aspect of life. It's about more than just guiding a team; it's about inspiring others, overcoming challenges, and continuously growing. From my early experiences in Mumbai and London to the various roles I've held, each step has taught me valuable lessons about what it means to lead. Leadership is about actions, not titles. It's about making a difference in the lives of those around you, no matter where you are or what role you play.

Poetic Reflection

As I pause to gather my thoughts, I find clarity in the rhythm of words. Leadership is not about power or status, but about the seeds of empathy we plant along the way.

In quiet moments, thoughts take flight,
Leadership blooms in acts of light.
Not a crown, nor a throne to claim,
But in kindness shown, it finds its name.

From the heart of a mother, firm and strong,
To a child who dares to right the wrong,
In friendships that weather time's own test,
And mentors who guide with wisdom's crest.

Leadership's journey is wide and deep,
In laughter shared and promises we keep.
It's in the rise after every fall,
In silent strength that answers the call.

May these words inspire and ignite,
A leader in you, with courage and might.
For in the end, it's what we do,
That shapes our world, both old and new.

In the end, leadership is about embracing your journey, learning from every experience, and using your unique strengths to make a positive impact.

Welcome to the Journey of Exploring the Many Faces of Leadership.

Chapter Two

The Human Side of Leadership

Leadership is not just about making decisions and driving results. It's about connecting with people, understanding their needs, and guiding them through challenges. It's about the human side of leadership, where empathy, compassion, and genuine care play pivotal roles.

The Foundation of Empathy

In the previous chapter, we explored the many faces of leadership, from the single mother juggling multiple jobs to the young activist fighting for change. Now, let's delve deeper into the foundation of effective leadership: empathy.

Empathy is the ability to understand and share the feelings of others. It's about putting yourself in someone else's shoes and seeing the world from their perspective. In leadership, empathy is crucial because it builds trust, fosters collaboration, and creates a supportive environment where everyone can thrive.

At its core, empathy is about connection. It's about recognising the emotions and experiences of others and responding with kindness and understanding. When leaders practice empathy, they create a sense of belonging and respect within their teams or communities. This connection is the bedrock of effective leadership because it encourages open communication, mutual respect, and a shared commitment to common goals.

Consider a simple example: imagine a team member who is consistently missing deadlines. A leader lacking empathy might respond with frustration or disciplinary action without understanding the underlying issues. In contrast, an empathetic leader would take the time to have a conversation, listen to the team member's concerns, and offer support. This approach not only addresses the immediate problem but also strengthens the relationship and fosters a more positive and productive work environment.

Empathy also involves being attuned to non-verbal cues. Often, what is left unsaid can be just as important as what is spoken. An empathetic leader notices these subtle signals and takes proactive steps to address them. This might mean offering a word of encouragement, providing additional resources, or simply being present and available to listen.

Empathy is not just about being nice; it's a powerful tool for effective problem-solving and innovation. When leaders understand the needs and challenges of their team members, they can make more informed decisions that benefit everyone. This understanding leads to better solutions and more innovative approaches because it incorporates diverse perspectives and experiences.

For example, consider a company facing a downturn in morale due to a stressful project. An empathetic leader would recognise the signs of burnout and take steps to alleviate stress, such as adjusting deadlines, providing mental health resources, or organising team-building activities. This proactive approach not only improves morale but also enhances productivity and creativity, leading to better outcomes for the project and the company as a whole.

Empathy is also essential in conflict resolution. When disagreements arise, an empathetic leader seeks to understand all sides of the issue before making decisions. This approach helps to defuse tension and find solutions that respect everyone's perspectives. By showing empathy, leaders demonstrate that they value each individual's input, which, in turn, fosters loyalty and commitment.

Moreover, empathy extends beyond immediate interactions. It shapes the overall culture of an organisation or community. Leaders who consistently model empathy create an environment where everyone feels valued and heard. This culture of empathy becomes self-reinforcing, as team members emulate the behaviour of their leaders, leading to a more cohesive and collaborative environment.

Empathy also plays a crucial role in personal growth. By understanding others, leaders gain insights into their own behaviours and attitudes. This self-awareness is a key component of emotional intelligence, which is essential for effective leadership. Leaders who are aware of their own emotions and how they impact others are better equipped to manage their teams and create positive change.

In summary, empathy is the foundation upon which effective leadership is built. It's about understanding and connecting with others, fostering an environment of trust and collaboration, and making informed decisions that benefit the whole. As we continue to explore the various aspects of leadership throughout this book, remember that empathy is the thread that weaves together all the qualities and actions of a great leader. It's the simple yet profound ability to see the world through the eyes of others and respond with kindness and understanding. This is the true essence of leadership, and it's a skill that we can all cultivate and nurture in our own lives.

My Journey with Empathy

My journey into empathetic leadership began long before I held any official title. As a young boy, I witnessed my mother's efforts to integrate into Mumbai's culture. Her resilience and determination were deeply rooted in her empathy for our family, teaching me the importance of understanding and supporting those around you.

When our family faced financial difficulties, I had to mature quickly. I took on various odd jobs to support myself and gain new experiences. Working as a salesman and retail cashier, I interacted with people from diverse backgrounds. These roles taught me the significance of listening, understanding, and responding to the needs of others. Each customer had a unique story, and by taking the time to listen, I formed connections that transcended mere transactions.

These experiences were instrumental in shaping my approach to leadership. They showed me that empathy is not just a trait, but a powerful tool for building trust and fostering meaningful relationships. As I progressed in my career, these early lessons remained at the core of my leadership philosophy, reminding me that empathy is the foundation of effective leadership.

One particularly memorable experience was during my time as a retail cashier. It was a busy holiday season, and the store was packed. People were stressed, and tempers were short. One day, an elderly woman came to my register, visibly frustrated because she couldn't find a particular item. She was upset and started to vent her frustrations at me.

Instead of reacting defensively, I took a deep breath and listened to her concerns. I assured her that I understood her frustration and would do my best to help. I left my post to personally assist her in finding the item. We found it together, and she thanked me profusely, her anger melting away.

Later that evening, my manager approached me. "I saw what you did for that customer today," he said. "That's the kind of attitude we need more of. You showed real leadership out there."

That moment was a revelation. It taught me that leadership isn't confined to high-level positions; it can be demonstrated in everyday actions, through empathy, and a willingness to help others.

Leading with Compassion

As I transitioned into more formal leadership roles, the early lessons in empathy I learned became invaluable. At 24, I was offered a position primarily due to my talent in finance. The company was experiencing rapid growth, but it lacked clear direction, cohesive processes, and strong leadership. It quickly became apparent that my responsibilities would extend far beyond managing numbers.

In my new role, I encountered a team that was struggling with low morale and high stress. They were talented individuals, but the lack of guidance and support had left them feeling disheartened. Drawing from my past experiences, I knew that empathy and compassion were key to turning things around. I made it a priority to understand their challenges and frustrations, taking the time to listen to each team member's concerns.

One of the first steps I took was to establish open communication channels. I initiated regular one-on-one meetings and team discussions, where everyone had the opportunity to voice their thoughts and ideas. This not only helped me understand their perspectives but also fostered a sense of belonging and trust within the team. By showing genuine interest in their well-being, I was able to build stronger connections and create a supportive work environment.

Beyond just listening, I took concrete actions to address the issues they faced. For instance, I noticed that the workload was unevenly distributed, causing burnout for some, while leaving others underutilised. I worked on restructuring the team's tasks to ensure a more balanced distribution of work. This not only alleviated stress but also empowered team members by matching their skills with appropriate responsibilities.

Additionally, I implemented initiatives aimed at professional development and personal growth. I encouraged team members to pursue training and educational opportunities that aligned with their career goals. By investing in their development, I demonstrated my commitment to their long-term success, which, in turn, boosted their confidence and motivation.

One particular instance that stands out is when a team member, Arjun, was going through a personal crisis. His performance had noticeably declined, and he seemed withdrawn. Instead of reprimanding him for his reduced productivity, I reached out to offer support. I assured him that his job was secure and encouraged him to take the time he needed to address his personal issues. This act of compassion not only helped Arjun regain his footing but also strengthened the trust and loyalty within the team.

Leading with compassion also meant recognising and celebrating the team's achievements. I made it a point to acknowledge their hard work and successes, both big and small. This created a positive feedback loop where team members felt valued and appreciated, further enhancing their commitment to the company's goals.

Through these efforts, I witnessed a transformation in the team's dynamics. The atmosphere shifted from one of uncertainty and frustration to one of collaboration and enthusiasm. The team became more cohesive, and their performance improved significantly. This experience reinforced my belief that empathy and compassion are not just nice-to-have qualities, but essential components of effective leadership.

My journey into formal leadership roles underscored the power of leading with compassion. By understanding and addressing the needs of my team, fostering open communication, and supporting their personal and professional growth, I was able to create a positive and productive work environment. These early lessons in empathy became the cornerstone of my leadership approach, guiding me in building strong, motivated, and resilient teams.

The Transformative Experience

From the moment I stepped into the office, I knew this job would be different. The company was chaotic, with departments operating in silos and a lack of clear communication. It was evident that they needed more than just a financial expert – they needed someone who could bring structure and vision.

In those early days, I felt a sense of ownership that went beyond my official title. It was almost as if I was helping to build the company from the ground up, nurturing it like a child. I spent countless hours understanding each department, identifying gaps, and working with the team to develop efficient processes.

One evening, while reviewing the quarterly reports, I realised the sheer volume of issues that needed addressing. The pressure was immense, but I felt a strange mix of anxiety and exhilaration. I saw potential in the chaos, an opportunity to make a real impact.

I remember calling a team meeting the next day. "We're all feeling the strain of growing pains," I began, looking around the room at faces weary from long hours and stress. "But I believe in this team, and I believe in what we're building here. Let's tackle these challenges together, step by step."

A New Approach

We started by implementing weekly inter-departmental meetings to improve communication and collaboration. I worked closely with team leaders to develop standardised processes and ensure that everyone was aligned with the company's goals. These changes weren't always easy, and there were moments of resistance and doubt.

One particularly challenging project was the overhaul of our inventory management system. It was outdated, leading to frequent stockouts and excess inventory. The IT team was sceptical about the proposed changes, fearing it would disrupt their workflow. I spent hours discussing their concerns, demonstrating the long-term benefits, and finding a middle ground.

During a late-night session, I sat down with Ravi, the head of IT. "I know this is a lot to take on," I said, "but think about the efficiencies we can achieve. This could streamline our operations and reduce a lot of the headaches we're currently facing."

Ravi nodded slowly. "Alright, let's give it a shot," he finally agreed. "But we'll need to be meticulous about the transition."

The project was arduous, but the results were transformative. Inventory accuracy improved dramatically, reducing costs and enhancing customer satisfaction. It was a testament to the power of collaboration and perseverance.

The Impact on Personal Growth

This job shaped me in ways I hadn't anticipated. It pushed me to develop skills in areas I hadn't previously explored and forced me to confront my own limitations. I learned the importance of flexibility, the value of different perspectives, and the necessity of balancing empathy with decisiveness.

Conversations that Shaped Leadership

A turning point in my leadership journey came during a conversation with Maya, a senior team member known for her wisdom and deep understanding of the company's culture. Maya had been with the company since its inception, earning respect through her unwavering commitment and her ability to navigate complex challenges with grace. She was not just a colleague but a mentor to many, including myself. Her insights were often sought after, and her ability to see the bigger picture, while caring deeply for her team, was unparalleled.

One day, we found ourselves discussing the growing pains and resistance to change that many employees were feeling. As someone who had witnessed the company's evolution from the ground up, Maya had a unique perspective on its strengths and areas needing improvement.

"Maya, you've been here from the start. What do you think we need to do to move forward?" I asked, genuinely seeking her counsel.

She looked at me thoughtfully, her eyes reflecting years of experience and understanding. "We need someone who can see the bigger picture, someone who cares about the people as much as the profits," she said. "I see that in you. But you need to trust yourself and trust us. We're all in this together."

Her words were a wake-up call. In that moment, I realised that leadership wasn't just about making the right decisions, but about believing in the collective strength of the team. Maya's wisdom reminded me that true leadership is about fostering an environment where everyone feels valued and heard, and where trust forms the foundation of all our efforts.

Maya's guidance has stayed with me ever since, shaping my approach to leadership and reinforcing the importance of empathy, trust, and collective effort. Her ability to balance vision with compassion continues to inspire me and serves as a benchmark for the kind of leader I strive to be.

My Current Job: A White Canvas

After spending several years in different cities around the world, I made the decision to move back to my hometown. It was a return to my roots, but also a leap into a new challenge. I took up a job at a company that, much like the one before, was in need of direction and leadership. The work environment was complex, and the challenges were immense. Yet, it felt like a blank canvas, waiting to be painted with fresh ideas and innovative solutions.

From the moment I joined, I saw the potential. The company had talent, but it needed structure, vision, and a cohesive culture.

I felt a deep sense of responsibility and opportunity. Here was a chance to apply everything I had learned over the years and build something remarkable from the ground up.

Building a New Culture

The first step was to create a culture of collaboration and trust. I introduced regular team-building activities and open forums where everyone could voice their ideas and concerns. These sessions were transformative. They broke down barriers and fostered a sense of unity and shared purpose.

One day, during an open forum, Prachi, a junior team member, spoke up. "I feel like we're all working in silos," she said. "We need more opportunities to collaborate and learn from each other."

Her honesty struck a chord with everyone in the room. "You're absolutely right, Prachi," I responded. "Let's work on creating more cross-functional projects and regular brainstorming sessions."

These changes started to take root. The team became more cohesive, and the flow of ideas and innovation increased. It was incredible to see the transformation. The company started to feel less like a workplace and more like a community, a place where everyone felt valued and empowered.

The Intersection of Talent and Opportunity

One key lesson I learned was that talent alone isn't enough; it needs to intersect with opportunity. This company provided that intersection, a place where I could apply my skills, learn from my experiences, and grow alongside my team.

During a strategy meeting, I shared this insight with my team. "We all have incredible talent here," I said. "But what makes us truly powerful is how we use these talents together, leveraging our opportunities to create something greater than the sum of its parts."

A Whiteboard Dream Realised

The journey wasn't easy. There were countless late nights, tough decisions, and moments of doubt. But each challenge brought us closer together and pushed us to innovate and improve. We built a company culture based on trust, efficiency, and mutual respect.

Looking back, it feels almost surreal. What started as a complex, fragmented work environment transformed into a cohesive, high-performing team. The culture and efficiency we have built are nothing short of incredible. It's a testament to the power of collective effort, empathy, and a shared vision.

A Place That Feels Like Home

This company became more than just a place of work; it became a home where we grew together, faced challenges together, and celebrated successes together. The sense of camaraderie and mutual respect we built was a testament to the culture we created, one that valued every individual's contribution and fostered a supportive environment.

Abhishek Bansal: The Visionary

I must credit a significant part of our success to Abhishek Bansal, the founder of our company. His vision and belief in me brought me to this place. Abhishek is a man of deep insight and relentless determination. From our first meeting, it was clear that he had a dream for the company that extended far beyond mere financial success.

"Abhishek, what drives you?" I asked him one late evening as we worked on refining our strategy.

He paused, looking thoughtfully out of the window. "I believe in the potential of people," he said. "When given the right environment, people can achieve extraordinary things. My goal is to create a space where everyone can thrive, where talent meets opportunity, and where innovation is a way of life."

His words resonated deeply with me. Abhishek's vision was not just about building a successful company, but about creating a community where every individual felt valued and empowered. This belief in people became the cornerstone of our culture, guiding us through every challenge and inspiring us to strive for excellence.

Learning Self-Motivation

In certain roles, especially in leadership, self-motivation is crucial. There were times when the path was unclear, when the weight of responsibility felt overwhelming, and quitting seemed like the easier option. But it was during these moments that I learned the true essence of self-motivation.

I often reminded myself of a quote by Harvey Spectre, a character from the TV show Suits: "I quit every day, I just never said it out loud. I would never give them the satisfaction of breaking me." This mindset helped me stay focused and driven, even when the going got tough.

One particularly challenging period was during the rollout of a new enterprise resource planning (ERP) system. The implementation was fraught with technical glitches, employee pushback, and unexpected delays. Every day presented a new obstacle, and there were moments when I questioned if we could pull it off.

One evening, after another long day, I sat in my office feeling defeated. Abhishek walked in, noticing my exhaustion. "Thinking about quitting?" he asked, half-jokingly.

"Every day," I replied with a tired smile.

"Good," he said, surprising me. "Because if you're not thinking about quitting, you're not pushing hard enough. But remember, it's about pushing through that feeling and coming out stronger on the other side."

His words stuck with me. They reminded me that leadership is about perseverance, about finding the strength to keep going, even when things seem impossible. It's about being self-motivated and inspiring that same determination in others.

The Virtues Developed

This journey has developed different virtues in me, bringing me closer to the version of myself I aspire to be. Patience, resilience, empathy, and the ability to inspire others have become integral parts of my leadership style. Each challenge we faced, and each success we celebrated, contributed to my growth as a leader and as a person.

I learned the importance of balancing empathy with decisiveness, of being firm yet compassionate. I realised that leadership is not about having all the answers, but about creating a space where others can find their answers and grow.

A Special Thanks to My Team

As I sit here, reflecting on the journey so far, I am filled with gratitude. This company, this team, has become my second family. Together, we have turned a whiteboard dream into reality, creating a culture and efficiency that we are all proud of.

Poetic Reflection: Embracing the Journey Together

Leadership is often seen as a solitary path, but in reality, it's a collective journey where each step we take together builds something greater than ourselves. This reflection captures the essence of our shared experiences, the challenges we've faced, and the unity we've cultivated.

In quiet corners where dreams were born,
We built our world each breaking dawn.
With every challenge, we found our pace,
A team united, strong in grace.

Through restless nights and tiring days,
Our strength emerged in subtle ways.
In every trial, a lesson deep,
In every setback, victories to keep.

This place of work has grown to be,
A home of shared reality.
Leadership is more than just a role—
It's how we've learned to make each whole.

Reflection and Vulnerability: The Leader's Path

In leadership, vulnerability is not a weakness but a source of strength. Reflecting on my journey, I've learned that true leadership is about embracing imperfections and being open to growth. This reflection encapsulates the lessons learned through moments of doubt and the strength found in empathy.

In chaos, I discovered my way,
Building dreams with each new day.
A leader, not by rank or choice,
But by empathy, giving voice.

Through trials faced and doubts unmasked,
I saw the strength in every task.
Leadership, a journey wide,
Shaped by hearts we stand beside.

Let's continue on this path we tread,
Empathetic leadership ahead.
For in the lives we touch and guide,
True leadership is realized.

As we move forward, let these insights not just guide us but also challenge us to redefine leadership—transforming it into a journey where empathy and resilience shape not only our actions but also the lasting impact we have on others.

Chapter Three

The Art of Listening

Leadership is often associated with commanding presence, decisive actions, and clear communication. However, one of the most overlooked yet vital components of effective leadership is the art of listening. Listening, when practiced with intention and empathy, transforms leaders into true connectors—individuals who not only lead but also understand, inspire, and guide others toward shared goals.

Listening as a Leadership Skill

Listening is often an underappreciated but crucial skill in leadership. It's not merely about hearing words; it's about understanding the deeper messages, emotions, and intentions behind them. In my journey, I have learned that effective listening can transform relationships, foster trust, and lead to more informed decisions.

In the hustle and bustle of leadership, it's easy to get caught up in the need to be heard, to assert one's ideas, and to drive decisions forward. Yet, the true strength of a leader often lies not in the words they speak, but in the ability to listen—really listen—to those around them. This is not just about hearing words; it's about understanding the unspoken, the emotions, and the motivations behind those words. It's about recognizing that every voice matters and that each person's perspective contributes to the bigger picture.

Great leaders know that listening is a powerful tool for building trust and fostering open communication within a team. When people feel heard, they feel valued, and this sense of value can significantly boost morale, creativity, and productivity. Listening shows respect, and respect breeds loyalty—one of the cornerstones of strong leadership.

The Transformative Power of Listening

In my early career, I worked under a manager who never seemed to listen. Meetings felt like one-way monologues, and team members rarely felt valued or understood. The atmosphere was tense, and productivity suffered. This experience taught me the importance of truly listening to those around me.

When I first stepped into a leadership role, I made it a priority to cultivate a culture of listening. I scheduled one-on-one meetings with team members, not just to discuss work, but to understand their personal goals, challenges, and aspirations. By actively listening, I was able to build stronger connections and foster a more cohesive and motivated team.

Listening is not just a passive activity—it's an active engagement with the world around us. It requires patience, humility, and a willingness to learn from others. When leaders listen, they open themselves up to a wealth of knowledge and ideas that can propel their teams and organizations forward.

Real-Life Examples: Transformative Listening

One of the most profound examples of listening comes from Howard Schultz, the former CEO of Starbucks. During the 2008 financial crisis, Schultz took the time to listen to his employees' concerns and ideas. This approach not only helped Starbucks navigate the crisis but also strengthened the company's culture and loyalty among its employees. Schultz often emphasizes that listening is an act of love and respect, which, in turn, creates a more engaged and dedicated workforce.

This example, among others, illustrates that listening is not just a leadership skill—it's a powerful tool that can transform an organization's culture, build trust, and drive success.

Techniques for Effective Listening

Listening effectively is a skill that can be developed with practice and intention. Here are some techniques that have proven invaluable in my leadership journey:

1. **Active Listening:** Engage fully with the speaker. This means maintaining eye contact, nodding, and providing feedback that shows understanding.
2. **Avoid Interrupting:** Let the speaker finish their thoughts before responding. Interruptions can make them feel undervalued.
3. **Ask Questions:** Clarify points and show interest by asking relevant questions.
4. **Paraphrase and Summarize:** Reflect back what you have heard to confirm understanding.
5. **Show Empathy:** Understand and acknowledge the speaker's feelings and perspectives.

These techniques have not only helped me become a better listener but have also fostered a more inclusive and trusting environment within my teams.

Personal Anecdote: Listening Transforms Team Dynamics

Early in my leadership career, I faced a significant challenge with a demoralized and skeptical team. Recognizing the importance of listening, I organized regular meetings where team members could voice their concerns and ideas. By actively listening and addressing their issues, we built a more cohesive and motivated team. This experience underscored the transformative power of listening in leadership.

One of the most poignant moments came when a team member, whom I'll call Sangeeta, finally opened up about her struggles balancing work and personal responsibilities. By listening and offering flexible work arrangements, not only did Sangeeta's performance improve, but she also became one of the most dedicated members of the team. This experience taught me that listening is not just about solving problems; it's about understanding people and creating an environment where they feel valued and supported.

Listening as a Philosophy

Listening is more than a skill; it's a philosophy. It's about valuing others, showing empathy, and creating a culture of openness and trust. As leaders, when we listen, we don't just hear words; we hear the heartbeat of our team. This understanding can drive us toward more effective and compassionate leadership.

Listening transforms leaders from mere decision-makers into visionaries who can inspire and guide their teams with a deep understanding of their needs and aspirations. It builds a culture of trust and respect, where people feel safe to express themselves and are motivated to do their best work.

A Poetic Reflection

As we close this chapter on the art of listening, it's fitting to reflect on the profound impact it can have on our leadership and our lives:

In the quiet of a listening ear,
A thousand voices find their voice.
In the patience of an open heart,
A thousand souls find their choice.

For in the art of truly hearing,
We build bridges strong and wide,
Connecting hearts and minds and spirits,
With trust and truth as our guide.

So listen not just with your ears,
But with the depth of your soul.
For in the space of silent moments,
Is where true leadership takes its toll.

Listening is the bridge that connects leadership with understanding, transforming actions into meaningful impact. As we continue to lead, let us remember that true power lies not in the words we speak, but in the moments we truly hear.

Chapter Four

The Heartbeat of Leadership

Leadership is a living, breathing force that pulsates through every interaction, decision, and moment of connection. It's not just about guiding a team or achieving goals; it's about touching the very core of human experience. The heartbeat of leadership lies in its ability to inspire, to connect, and to make people believe in themselves. This chapter explores the transformative power of heartfelt leadership through stories and experiences that bring the essence of leadership to life.

What is the heartbeat of leadership? It's the intangible rhythm that drives leaders to inspire others, to see potential where others see limitations, and to foster growth in those around them. It's about leading with empathy, compassion, and genuine care. The heartbeat of leadership is felt in the moments when we connect with others on a deeper level, transforming lives through our words and actions.

Rahul: Giving Wings to Fly

Rahul was a quiet worker, remarkable at his job, but often confined to his role as an individual contributor. He had immense talent, but his reserved nature kept him from stepping into leadership roles. I saw potential in Rahul that went beyond his current contributions.

One day, after a particularly successful project, I called Rahul into my office. "Rahul, you did an outstanding job on this project," I began. "Have you ever thought about taking on more leadership responsibilities?"

He looked surprised. "I've always preferred working independently," he admitted. "I'm not sure if I'm cut out for leadership."

"I see something in you, Rahul. You have the skills and the dedication, but more importantly, you have the respect of your colleagues. Leadership isn't just about directing others; it's about inspiring them through your example. Let's work together to help you develop these skills."

Over the next few months, we focused on building Rahul's confidence and leadership abilities. I encouraged him to take the lead on small projects, gradually increasing his responsibilities. With each success, his confidence grew. Rahul transformed from a quiet worker to an accomplished leader, guiding his team with a blend of humility and determination. Seeing his transformation was a testament to the power of belief and the impact of heartfelt leadership.

Shanti: Valuing Experience

Shanti, the oldest employee in our company, had dedicated her life to her work. Her years of experience were invaluable, but she often felt overshadowed by younger, more dynamic colleagues. I noticed her hesitance to voice her ideas during meetings, despite her wealth of knowledge.

One afternoon, I invited Shanti for a coffee. "Shanti, your experience and insights are incredibly valuable to our team. I've noticed you often hold back during discussions. What can we do to make you feel more comfortable sharing your ideas?"

She smiled warmly. "I've always felt that my way of thinking might be considered outdated, compared to the younger generation."

"Your perspective is unique and vital," I assured her. "We need your wisdom to guide us. Let's find a way for you to mentor some of the newer employees and share your knowledge."

With this new role, Shanti flourished. She became a mentor to younger team members, her confidence grew, and she began contributing more actively in meetings. By valuing her experience and encouraging her to share it, we not only boosted her confidence, but also enriched our team with her insights.

Sheriar: Sharpening Skills

Sheriar was a young, enthusiastic recruit who joined us as a fresher. He had the raw talent and drive but lacked the communication skills to effectively convey his ideas. I saw a natural leader in him, someone who could inspire others if given the right guidance.

"Sheriar, you have incredible potential," I told him during one of our one-on-one sessions. "Let's work on sharpening your communication skills so you can effectively share your vision with others."

We started with small steps – technical skills, inter-department exposure, and regular feedback sessions. Sheriar was eager to learn and put in the effort to improve. Gradually, his confidence grew, and he began to own the floor during meetings. Today, Sheriar is a natural leader, commanding respect and inspiring his colleagues with his clear vision and effective communication.

These stories illustrate the heartbeat of leadership – the deep connection that transforms individuals and helps them realise their potential. But how do you recognise this heartbeat? How do you stay connected to it? Is it the genuine desire to see others succeed?

Recognising the Heartbeat

Recognising the heartbeat of leadership is not always straightforward. It's felt in moments of genuine connection and understanding, in the encouraging words that lift someone's spirits, in the opportunities we create for others to shine, and in the trust we build through our actions. But it's more than just these actions; it's about empathy, active listening, and a genuine desire to see others succeed.

Staying Connected to the Heart

Staying connected to the heartbeat of leadership involves continuous self-reflection and a commitment to leading with authenticity. This process is not easy and is often fraught with personal vulnerabilities and challenges. As leaders, we are human too, and balancing the ideal of an empowered team with our own imperfections can be daunting.

Self-reflection often begins with denial. When faced with feedback, especially critical feedback, the initial reaction might be to reject it. We might think, "That's not me," or "They don't understand the pressures I'm under." But over time, if we allow ourselves to be open, these reflections can lead to deeper understanding and growth.

I remember feeling overwhelmed by the demands of leadership, questioning my decisions, and facing moments of self-doubt. In those times, feedback felt like an attack rather than a helpful insight. However, as I slowly opened up to these perspectives, I began to see the truth in them. The stages of self-reflection—denial, resistance, acceptance, and finally, growth—are crucial. Each stage brings its own set of emotions and realisations.

During one particular period of self-doubt, I found myself grappling with a piece of feedback that suggested I wasn't as approachable as I believed. Initially, I was defensive. How could they think that? I prided myself on being open and supportive. But as I reflected more deeply, I began to see moments where I might have unintentionally created barriers.

This realisation was painful but necessary. It pushed me to make conscious changes in my behaviour – becoming more present in conversations, actively seeking input from my team, and making a genuine effort to show that I valued their contributions. These changes didn't happen overnight, and there were setbacks along the way. But each step forward, no matter how small, was a move towards becoming a more empathetic and effective leader.

Leadership is about being present in the moment, understanding the needs and aspirations of those we lead, and fostering an environment where everyone feels valued and empowered. It's a continuous journey of balancing our own vulnerabilities with the needs of our team. It's about striving for that ideal world where everyone can succeed, while acknowledging that the path to get there is filled with personal challenges and growth.

In the end, staying connected to the heartbeat of leadership means embracing our humanity, being willing to learn and grow, and always keeping the genuine desire to see others succeed at the forefront of our actions. It's not a textbook lesson, but a lived experience, full of complexities and triumphs, that shapes who we are as leaders.

The Philosophical Heart of Leadership

Leadership, at its core, is a philosophical endeavour. It's about understanding the interconnectedness of human experiences and recognising that our actions have a ripple effect on those around us. The heartbeat of leadership is the realisation that by touching one life, we can inspire a chain reaction of positive change.

As I reflect on my journey, I am reminded of the profound impact that words and actions can have on individuals. By believing in people, providing them with opportunities, and guiding them with empathy, we can create environments where everyone thrives.

A Poetic Reflection

As we close this chapter, let's reflect on the essence of leadership through poetry:

In the rhythm of our daily strife, leadership breathes, giving life. Not in titles or in tasks, but in the faces behind the masks.

> *A gentle word, a guiding hand, turns doubts to dreams, like shifting sand. In hearts we touch, in lives we mould, the true essence of leadership unfolds.*
>
> *Through belief and trust, we pave the way, inspiring others day by day. For in each soul, a spark ignites when touched by a leader with heart and light.*

Every leader's journey is unique, marked by the lives they touch and the hearts they inspire. Let's carry this essence forward as we continue to explore the many facets of leadership in the chapters ahead.

Chapter Five

Ambition - The Fire and the Burn

Ambition is a powerful force, a fire that burns within, driving us to strive for more, to push beyond our limits, and to achieve greatness. But like any fire, ambition can be both a source of warmth and light, or a consuming blaze that leaves us burnt. This chapter explores the dual nature of ambition, offering examples of both its inspiring potential and its dangerous pitfalls, and highlighting the importance of balanced ambition with clear intentions and direction.

The Spark of Ambition

Ambition often starts with a spark, a moment of realisation that ignites a desire for something greater. For many, this spark comes from a deep-seated drive to overcome adversity, achieve personal goals, or make a meaningful impact.

For me, the spark of ambition was ignited during a pivotal moment in my childhood. At the age of 13, my family faced financial ruin. The stability and comfort I had known vanished overnight, leaving me with a profound sense of uncertainty. My situation fuelled a fierce determination to change my circumstances. The abandonment and uncertainty I experienced became the fuel for my ambition, driving me to excel academically and professionally.

Inspiring Examples of Ambition

Ambition is often a response to challenging circumstances, a force that propels individuals to break barriers and achieve what seems impossible.

Rising from Adversity: Oprah Winfrey

Oprah Winfrey's journey is a prime example of ambition fuelled by a desire to overcome adversity. Born into poverty and facing numerous hardships, Oprah's ambition drove her to become one of the most influential media personalities in the world. Her determination to succeed, combined with her ability to connect with audiences on a deep, emotional level, transformed her life and inspired millions of others.

Innovating for Change: Elon Musk

Elon Musk's ambition is characterised by his relentless pursuit of innovation and change. From founding PayPal to revolutionising space travel with SpaceX, and transforming the automotive industry with Tesla, Musk's ambition is driven by a clear vision of the future. His bold, often risky endeavours exemplify how ambition can lead to groundbreaking advancements when channelled with clear intentions and direction.

Balancing Personal and Professional Goals: Indra Nooyi

Indra Nooyi, former CEO of PepsiCo, is an example of balanced ambition. Her career is marked by significant professional achievements, including leading PepsiCo through a period of transformation and growth. At the same time, Nooyi has been vocal about the importance of balancing personal and professional goals, advocating for family-friendly policies and work-life balance. Her approach demonstrates that ambition can be both powerful and sustainable when guided by clear intentions and a holistic view of success.

The Dark Side of Ambition

While ambition can drive positive change, it also has a darker side. When unchecked, it can lead to destructive behaviours and negative outcomes.

The Perils of Unchecked Ambition: Elizabeth Holmes

Elizabeth Holmes, founder of Theranos, provides a cautionary tale of ambition gone awry. Driven by a desire to revolutionise the healthcare industry, Holmes made bold claims about her company's technology that were later revealed to be false. Her relentless pursuit of success, without ethical considerations, ultimately led to the downfall of Theranos and significant legal consequences. This example underscores the importance of integrity and accountability in ambitious pursuits.

The Cost of Overambition: Bernie Madoff

Bernie Madoff's story is a stark reminder of how overambition can lead to devastating consequences. Madoff's ambition to maintain his status and wealth led him to create one of the largest Ponzi schemes in history. His actions caused immense financial harm to countless individuals and organisations, illustrating how unchecked ambition can have far-reaching negative impacts.

My Own Journey: Ambition Fuelled by Circumstance

My ambition was not born from a desire for wealth or status, but from a need to overcome adversity and provide security for my family. Growing up in a financially unstable environment ignited a fire within me, pushing me to rise above my circumstances. This drive has been a constant force throughout my life, evolving over time to encompass not just personal success, but also personal growth and making a meaningful impact.

As a young boy, I dreamed of becoming an automobile engineer. While life took me on a different path, the essence of that dream—innovation, creation, and striving for excellence—remained with me. Every step of my journey, from securing a visa to study in London, to navigating various odd jobs, taught me invaluable lessons about resilience, hard work, and adaptability. These experiences were instrumental in shaping my character and fortifying my resolve.

Over time, my ambition grew beyond mere financial stability. It became about personal growth, making a difference, and creating a legacy. This evolution was marked by pivotal moments and challenges that required me to step out of my comfort zone and embrace new opportunities. Each role I took on, whether as a leader in a struggling company or in any other capacity, was driven by a clear vision and unwavering determination to make a positive impact.

Living part of my dream at any given moment was a crucial realisation. It taught me to appreciate the journey and the progress made, while still striving for more. Ambition, I learned, is not a static goal, but a dynamic force that evolves with time. It is about acknowledging the journey, appreciating the present, and continuously aiming for greater heights.

In essence, my ambition is fuelled by a blend of overcoming adversity, striving for personal and professional growth, and making a meaningful impact. This journey, while filled with challenges, has been a testament to the power of resilience and the importance of living parts of our dream at each stage of life.

Balanced Ambition in Leadership

Balanced ambition involves pursuing goals with clear intentions and ethical considerations. It's about striving for success, while maintaining integrity, accountability, and a sense of purpose.

Ethical Leadership: Satya Nadella

Satya Nadella, CEO of Microsoft, exemplifies balanced ambition. Under his leadership, Microsoft has seen significant growth and innovation. Nadella's approach focuses on empathy, collaboration, and a growth mindset, ensuring that the company's ambition aligns with its values and ethical standards. His leadership style highlights the importance of fostering a positive culture and driving success with a clear, ethical vision.

Ambition in Action: Stories of Transformation

Ambition, when channelled positively, can lead to profound personal and professional growth. Here's a story from my journey that illustrates the power of ambition and the importance of letting go to foster growth.

Vikas: A Journey of Self-Discovery

Vikas was one of my most promising mentees. From the moment I joined the company, it was clear he had an incredible drive and potential. Over the years, I had the privilege of mentoring him, helping him navigate the complexities of our work environment, and guiding him as he developed his skills and confidence.

Vikas was diligent and eager to learn. He took on every challenge with enthusiasm and quickly rose through the ranks. However, as time went on, I noticed a growing restlessness in him. One evening, after a particularly intense day at work, Vikas asked to speak with me.

"Bhai (brother), I've been thinking a lot about my future," he began, looking uncertain. "I've learned so much under your guidance, but I feel like I'm starting to rely too much on your support. The more I stay under your umbrella, the less I'll learn how to keep myself dry."

His words struck a chord with me. While it hurt to hear that he wanted to leave, I understood his need to find his own path. Ambition, after all, is not just about achieving success, but also about personal growth and self-discovery.

"I understand, Vikas," I replied, feeling a mix of pride and sadness. "Sometimes, the best way to grow is to step out of your comfort zone. If you feel this is what you need to do, I support you fully. Just know that you always have a mentor and a friend in me."

Vikas's decision to leave was driven by his ambition to find himself, to step out of the shadows, and learn to navigate the challenges on his own. It was a difficult goodbye, but watching him take that bold step towards his own growth was incredibly rewarding. Vikas went on to achieve great things, applying the lessons he had learned and forging his own path with confidence and determination.

The Fire and the Burn of Ambition

Vikas's story highlights the dual nature of ambition. On one hand, it drives us to seek new opportunities, to push beyond our limits, and to achieve greatness. On the other hand, it can lead to difficult decisions and sacrifices, often requiring us to step away from familiar support systems to truly grow.

Balanced Ambition in Leadership

Balanced ambition involves pursuing goals with clear intentions and ethical considerations. It's about striving for success, while maintaining integrity, accountability, and a sense of purpose.

In my professional life, balanced ambition meant recognising when to guide and when to let go, understanding that true mentorship sometimes involves giving people the freedom to find their own way. It's about fostering an environment where individuals can grow, learn, and eventually spread their wings.

The Philosophical Heart of Ambition

Ambition, at its core, is about more than achieving personal success. It's about understanding the broader impact of our actions and striving to make a positive difference. The heartbeat of ambition is the realisation that our goals should align with a higher purpose, creating value, not just for ourselves, but for others as well.

Reflection and Growth

As we reflect on stories of ambition, it becomes evident that success is not merely about reaching the top, but about the journey and the impact we have along the way. True ambition should be guided by integrity, empathy, and a steadfast commitment to ethical principles.

Reflecting on my own journey, I realise that my ambition was fuelled not just by a desire for personal success, but by a need to provide security for my family and to prove to myself that I could rise above my circumstances. The challenges I faced and the lessons I learned have profoundly shaped my understanding of ambition, teaching me the importance of balance and ethical considerations.

One particular instance stands out vividly – a period when I was overwhelmed by the pressures of my role and felt paralysed by the fear of failure. It was a bottleneck that affected not only my professional drive but also my personal confidence. During this time, I was forced to confront my vulnerabilities and reassess my approach. The intense self-doubt and discouragement made me question my abilities and the path I had chosen. This deadlock slowed down the fire within me, making me wonder if I could truly succeed.

Overcoming this period of self-doubt was not easy. It required deep introspection and a willingness to seek support and guidance. I turned to mentors, friends, and family who believed in me, even when I struggled to believe in myself. Their encouragement and honest feedback helped me see my situation from a new perspective.

I learned that self-doubt is a natural part of the journey and that overcoming it requires perseverance and a willingness to seek support. Reflecting on this period now, I see it as a critical turning point that strengthened my resolve and deepened my understanding of what it means to pursue ambition with integrity.

Through each bottleneck and moment of self-doubt, I emerged stronger and more determined, with a clearer vision of what I wanted to achieve and how I wanted to achieve it. These experiences taught me that ambition is not a linear path, but a series of peaks and valleys. The setbacks and challenges are just as important as the successes because they provide the opportunity for growth and self-discovery.

In conclusion, ambition should be about more than just personal success. It should encompass the journey, the impact on others, and the unwavering adherence to ethical principles. My experiences have shown me that true growth comes from navigating through difficulties, reflecting on our motivations, and continuously striving to align our ambitions with our values. This reflective process not only fuels our drive but also ensures that our pursuit of success is meaningful and sustainable.

A Poetic Reflection: The Flame of Ambition

Ambition shapes every chapter of our lives, guiding our steps and igniting our path. This reflection captures the essence of ambition in leadership:

In the embers of the past, a fire is born,
A spark that lights the darkest morn.
Through trials faced and fears untold,
A beacon burns, a story unfolds.

Ambition drives with steady might,
Not for wealth or fleeting light,
But for the tales that time will spin,
Of battles fought and victories within.

In this fire, our path is clear,
Through the burn, we persevere.
For ambition's flame, both fierce and bright,
Leads us through the shadowed night.

Ambition is not just about what we achieve, but about how we grow through the journey. When aligned with integrity and purpose, it becomes a force that helps us overcome obstacles and elevate those around us. As we move forward, let us ensure our pursuit of success is always guided by empathy, wisdom, and a commitment to a greater good.

Chapter Six

The Shadow of Insecurity

Insecurity is an insidious shadow that can creep into the lives of leaders, influencing their decisions, behaviours, and relationships. It is a force that can undermine confidence, create doubt, and lead to a host of challenges, both personally and professionally. This chapter delves into the pervasive nature of insecurity, its impact on leadership, and the lessons learned from encountering insecure leaders.

The Nature of Insecurity

Insecurity stems from a lack of self-assurance and a fear of inadequacy. It manifests in various ways, from doubting one's abilities to feeling threatened by others' successes. For leaders, insecurity can be particularly damaging, as it affects not only their own performance but also the morale and productivity of their teams. This insecurity often leads to micromanagement, withholding of praise, and creating an environment where employees feel undervalued and unappreciated.

The fear of being exposed as inadequate can drive leaders to act defensively, avoiding risks and innovation. They might shy away from making bold decisions, fearing failure and judgement. This conservative approach can stifle creativity and growth within the team, leading to stagnation. Additionally, insecure leaders may struggle with giving credit where it's due, as they fear that recognising others' contributions might overshadow their own.

Encountering an Insecure Leader

One of the most profound lessons I learned about insecurity in leadership came from my encounter with an insecure boss. He was a capable leader, but his deep-seated insecurities cast a shadow over his leadership style. This experience taught me invaluable lessons about the importance of self-awareness and the impact of insecurity on team dynamics.

The Insecure Boss

This leader, let's call him Raj, was always worried about my work being acknowledged. Whenever I achieved something noteworthy, he downplayed my contributions or took credit for my ideas. His insecurity made him feel threatened by my successes, and he often held me back from opportunities that could have furthered my career. Raj's actions were not malicious, but stemmed from a deep fear of being outshone. He believed that acknowledging my contributions would somehow diminish his own accomplishments.

Working under Raj was stifling. My motivation dwindled, and my confidence took a hit. I felt like I was shrinking, unable to grow or express my true potential. Every day felt like walking on eggshells, trying not to outshine my boss, while still striving to do my best work. It was a challenging period, but it also taught me valuable lessons about the importance of finding a supportive leader and the impact of transparency in leadership.

In this environment, the lack of recognition and constant need to minimise my achievements began to affect my self-esteem. I found myself second-guessing my decisions and doubting my abilities. This experience highlighted the critical role leaders play in fostering a positive work culture and the detrimental effects of insecurity on employee morale.

Over time, I began to understand that Raj's behaviour was not personal. His insecurities were deeply rooted in his own experiences and fears. Raj had risen through the ranks in a highly competitive environment where mistakes were unforgivable, and recognition was scarce. This upbringing had conditioned him to see others' successes as threats, rather than opportunities for collaboration and growth. He viewed his position as constantly under threat, leading him to act defensively and protectively.

Understanding Raj's background gave me a new perspective on his actions. It made me realise that his need to assert dominance and control was a manifestation of his own insecurities. This insight allowed me to approach him with empathy, recognising that he was struggling with his own fears and doubts.

Recognising this, I started to view Raj with empathy. He was a product of his environment, doing his best to navigate his own fears and insecurities. His actions were more a reflection of his internal struggles than a deliberate attempt to undermine me. This realisation helped me see the situation from a different perspective and approach it with a sense of understanding, rather than resentment.

Instead of reacting with frustration, I began to approach our interactions with patience and compassion. I sought to understand his perspective and find common ground. This shift in mindset not only improved our working relationship, but also helped me develop a deeper sense of empathy and emotional intelligence.

Overcoming Impostor Syndrome

While I was fortunate enough to feel gratitude for every step forward in my career, impostor syndrome still made an appearance. Impostor syndrome is the belief that one's success is due to luck rather than skill, and that one will eventually be exposed as a fraud. It's a common feeling among high achievers and can undermine even the most genuine accomplishments.

Acknowledging the Feelings

The first step in overcoming impostor syndrome was acknowledging its presence. I had to accept that these feelings of inadequacy were part of my experience and not a reflection of my actual capabilities. Recognising that many successful people experience similar doubts was a crucial realisation. This acknowledgement allowed me to confront these feelings head-on, rather than letting them fester in the background.

I found solace in reading about the experiences of other high achievers who had faced similar challenges. Their stories provided reassurance that these feelings were normal and not indicative of my actual abilities. This shift in perspective helped me to view my accomplishments more objectively and to recognise my strengths.

Seeking Feedback

I began seeking constructive feedback from trusted mentors and colleagues. Hearing their perspectives helped me see my strengths more clearly and provided a more balanced view of my performance. Their positive reinforcement and honest critiques were invaluable in rebuilding my confidence. This feedback loop became an essential part of my growth, allowing me to continuously improve and gain a better understanding of my abilities.

Additionally, I started keeping a journal to document my achievements and reflect on my progress. This practice helped me to internalise my successes and build a stronger sense of self-assurance. Over time, these strategies helped me to manage and mitigate the impact of impostor syndrome on my professional life.

Transforming Insecure Leadership

Encountering insecure leaders can be challenging, but there are ways to navigate, and even transform, these situations for your own growth.

Building Your Own Confidence

Working under an insecure leader like Raj taught me to build my own confidence from within. Instead of relying solely on external validation, I learned to trust my abilities and accomplishments. I focused on personal growth and continuous learning, which helped me stay motivated, despite the lack of recognition from my boss. This internal shift allowed me to reclaim my sense of self-worth and to view challenges as opportunities for growth.

I began setting personal goals and celebrating my achievements, no matter how small. This practice reinforced my self-confidence and helped me to maintain a positive outlook, even in the face of adversity. By taking ownership of my development, I was able to thrive, despite the challenging environment.

Finding Supportive Mentors

Finding mentors who were secure in their own leadership and willing to invest in my development was crucial. These mentors provided the guidance and encouragement that Raj couldn't offer. They celebrated my successes and offered constructive criticism, helping me grow both personally and professionally. Their support was instrumental in my journey, providing a source of stability and encouragement.

Mentorship also taught me the importance of seeking diverse perspectives. Engaging with mentors from different backgrounds and industries broadened my understanding and enriched my professional experience. This network of support helped me to navigate the complexities of my career with greater confidence and resilience.

Creating a Positive Environment

As I progressed in my career, I made it a priority to create a positive and supportive environment for my own team. I wanted to be the kind of leader who celebrated others' successes and provided opportunities for growth. Transparency and trust became the cornerstones of my leadership style, fostering a culture where everyone felt valued and empowered. This approach not only enhanced team morale but also drove innovation and collaboration.

I implemented regular feedback sessions and team-building activities to strengthen our relationships and ensure open communication. By fostering an environment of mutual respect and support, I was able to cultivate a high-performing team that thrived on collaboration and shared success.

Learning from Insecurity

One of the most valuable lessons I learned from dealing with insecure leadership is the importance of creating a supportive and empowering work environment. I realised that the best leaders are those who lift others up, who are not threatened by their team's successes, but celebrate them.

Encouraging Growth

Encouraging growth in my team became a priority. I focused on providing opportunities for learning and development, recognising that when team members grow, the entire organisation benefits. This approach not only improved team morale, but also fostered a culture of continuous improvement and innovation.

I introduced professional development programmes and encouraged team members to pursue further education and training. By investing in their growth, I demonstrated my commitment to their success and created a pathway for continuous advancement.

Promoting Transparency

Promoting transparency in all interactions was another key lesson. By being open about challenges and successes, and by providing clear and honest feedback, I created an environment where trust could flourish. This transparency helped to build stronger relationships within the team, and increased overall engagement and productivity.

Regular team meetings and open forums allowed for candid discussions and collaborative problem-solving. This approach ensured that everyone felt heard and valued, fostering a sense of unity and shared purpose.

Insecurity in Life and Relationships

Insecurity isn't limited to professional settings; it also permeates our personal lives and relationships. Just as an insecure leader can stifle growth, an insecure partner can create an environment of doubt and mistrust.

Recognising Insecurity

Recognising insecurity in ourselves and others is the first step towards addressing it. In relationships, insecurity can manifest as jealousy, possessiveness, and constant reassurance-seeking. These behaviours stem from a fear of inadequacy and can erode the foundation of trust and respect in a partnership.

Identifying these patterns in ourselves and our partners allows us to address the root causes and work towards healthier dynamics. Open communication and mutual understanding are essential in overcoming these challenges and building stronger relationships.

Building Healthy Relationships

Building healthy relationships involves fostering an environment of mutual trust and support. Just as in professional settings, transparency and open communication are key. Partners should encourage each other's growth, celebrate successes, and provide a safe space for expressing vulnerabilities.

Regular check-ins and honest conversations about fears and insecurities can strengthen the bond between partners. By acknowledging and addressing these issues, couples can build a foundation of trust and mutual respect, fostering a healthy and supportive relationship.

The Philosophical Heart of Insecurity

Insecurity is a deeply human experience. It challenges us, shapes us, and ultimately teaches us resilience. Embracing our insecurities and learning from them can lead to profound personal and professional growth.

Insecurity pushes us to confront our vulnerabilities and seek growth. It reminds us that we are all imperfect, and that true strength lies in our ability to acknowledge and learn from our flaws. By embracing our insecurities, we can transform them into sources of strength and resilience.

A Poetic Reflection

Insecurity in leadership can be a silent yet powerful force, shaping our decisions and interactions in ways we may not always realize. This poem seeks to capture the essence of that struggle, and how, through empathy and support, we can transform insecurity into strength.

In shadows deep, where doubts abide,
Insecurity seeks to divide.
A heart that quakes, fearing the fall,
Yet rises strong, standing tall.

Through clouds of doubt, a light appears,
Igniting hope, dispelling fears.
In flaws, our truths are often found,
A leader's wounds, where healing's bound.

To those who falter, lend your hand,
Build a shelter, help them stand.
With words of kindness, acts of grace,
Lift them up, their fears efface.

In every soul, a seed of might,
When nurtured well, takes flight in light.
Through empathy, we weave a thread,
Of strength and hope, where fears are shed.

Together rising, hearts entwined,
In shelter given, peace we find.
For on this path, where we confide,
Insecurity, we can deride.

Through leadership that shares and cares,
A brighter future, each prepares.

Insecurity is a shadow that can cloud our judgement and stifle our growth. But by recognising and addressing it, we can transform it into a source of strength and resilience. As we continue this journey of self-discovery and leadership, let us remember that true strength lies in acknowledging our vulnerabilities and using them as a catalyst for growth, and in providing a shelter of support and encouragement for others.

Chapter Seven

The Power of Vulnerability

Leadership is often associated with strength, authority, and decisiveness. However, one of the most overlooked and underappreciated qualities of effective leadership is vulnerability. Embracing vulnerability can transform leadership, foster deeper connections, and create an environment where trust and authenticity flourish. This chapter explores the power of vulnerability in leadership and how it can be a catalyst for growth, innovation, and stronger relationships.

Embracing Vulnerability

Vulnerability is often seen as a weakness, something to be hidden or avoided. Yet, in reality, it is a source of strength and courage. By embracing vulnerability, leaders can show their authentic selves, admitting to their own fears, doubts, and mistakes. This openness invites others to do the same, breaking down barriers and building trust.

The Courage to Be Real

One of the most profound moments in my leadership journey came when I decided to share a personal failure with my team. I had made a significant mistake in a project that cost the company both time and resources. Instead of covering it up or shifting the blame, I chose to own my mistake and discuss it openly with my team.

"I made a mistake," I began, addressing my team with a heavy heart. "This project didn't go as planned because of a decision I made. I take full responsibility for it, and I want us to learn from this experience together."

The response was overwhelming. Instead of losing respect, my team rallied around me. They appreciated my honesty and saw my vulnerability as a sign of strength. It created an environment where they felt safe to share their own challenges and failures, knowing that it was okay to make mistakes and learn from them. This moment was a turning point, reinforcing the idea that true leadership involves transparency and authenticity.

Building Trust Through Vulnerability

Trust is the foundation of any successful team. When leaders show vulnerability, it humanises them and breaks down the invisible walls that often separate them from their team members. This openness fosters a culture of trust, where everyone feels valued and understood.

Creating a Safe Space

One of my colleagues, Priya, was struggling with a personal issue that was affecting her performance at work. I noticed her distress and invited her for a private conversation.

"Priya, I've noticed you've been a bit off lately. Is there anything you'd like to talk about?" I asked, genuinely concerned.

She hesitated at first, but then opened up about her difficulties. By creating a safe space and showing empathy, I was able to support her through a tough time. This experience reinforced the importance of vulnerability in building trust and supporting team members in their personal and professional lives. By acknowledging her struggles, I was able to provide the necessary support and resources to help her navigate through her challenges.

The Innovation That Comes From Vulnerability

Innovation thrives in environments where people feel safe to express their ideas, take risks, and challenge the status quo. Vulnerability plays a crucial role in fostering such environments.

Encouraging Creative Risk-Taking

During a brainstorming session, I encouraged my team to share bold and unconventional ideas. "There are no bad ideas here," I told them. "Let's think outside the box and see where it takes us."

One of the junior members hesitated before sharing a radical idea. It was met with mixed reactions, but instead of dismissing it, we explored it further. This openness to vulnerability and risk-taking led to a breakthrough solution that significantly improved our processes. By fostering a culture where it was safe to take risks, we unlocked new levels of creativity and innovation.

The Strength in Asking for Help

Leaders are often expected to have all the answers, but no one can be an expert in everything. Asking for help is a powerful demonstration of vulnerability and humility.

The Lesson of Collaboration

I once faced a complex challenge that was beyond my expertise. Instead of struggling alone, I reached out to a colleague known for her expertise in that area.

"Can you help me with this?" I asked, feeling a bit exposed.

Her willingness to assist, and our subsequent collaboration, not only solved the problem but also strengthened our working relationship. This experience taught me that asking for help is not a sign of weakness, but a demonstration of strength and trust in others' abilities. It highlighted the value of collaboration and the collective power of diverse perspectives.

The Ripple Effect of Vulnerability

Vulnerability in leadership doesn't just affect the leader; it has a ripple effect throughout the organisation. When leaders model vulnerability, it encourages a culture where everyone feels comfortable being their authentic selves.

Fostering Authentic Relationships

By being open and vulnerable, leaders can foster genuine relationships within their teams. These relationships are built on mutual respect, trust, and understanding, leading to higher morale, better collaboration, and increased productivity. Authentic connections, fostered through vulnerability, can lead to a more cohesive and motivated team.

> ### A Poetic Reflection on Vulnerability
>
> Reflecting on the power of vulnerability, I find solace and inspiration in poetry. Here's a piece that captures the essence of vulnerability in leadership:
>
> *In the openness of a fragile heart lies the strength that sets us apart. To lead with truth, to show our fears, builds bonds of trust through honest tears.*
>
> *In every flaw, in each mistake, the seeds of growth, we softly wake. For in the courage to be seen, we find the power to truly glean.*
>
> *From hidden depths, our strengths arise. In vulnerability, we realise. The leaders who dare to show their soul inspire others to feel whole.*
>
> *Through shared stories, trust is spun. In the light of truth, we become one.*

Vulnerability is not a weakness; it is a profound source of strength and connection. As we continue this journey of self-discovery and leadership, let us embrace vulnerability as a powerful tool to build trust, foster innovation, and create meaningful relationships. By showing our true selves, we can inspire others to do the same, leading to a more authentic and connected world.

Chapter Eight

The Loneliness of Leadership

Leadership is often glorified as a position of power, influence, and respect. However, one of the less discussed aspects of leadership is the profound loneliness that can accompany it. Being at the top can feel isolating, with the weight of decisions and responsibilities often leaving leaders feeling alone. This chapter delves into the loneliness of leadership, the challenges it presents, and ways to overcome this pervasive feeling.

The Inevitable Isolation

One of the most challenging aspects of leadership is the sense of isolation that can come with it. Leaders often find themselves at a distance from their teams, colleagues, and even peers due to the nature of their role. The higher you rise, the fewer peers you have who truly understand the unique pressures and responsibilities you face.

The Distance from Teams

As leaders ascend the organisational hierarchy, they naturally move away from day-to-day interactions with their teams. This physical and emotional distance can create a barrier to understanding the daily challenges and dynamics that their team members experience. While leaders strive to maintain open lines of communication, the sheer scale of their responsibilities often means they cannot be as intimately involved as they once were.

For instance, a CEO overseeing thousands of employees across multiple locations cannot have the same level of personal interaction with every team member as a frontline manager might. This separation can lead to a sense of disconnection, making it difficult for leaders to gauge the true sentiment and morale within their organisation. They rely heavily on reports, metrics, and feedback from middle management, which can sometimes be filtered or diluted.

The Isolation from Colleagues

Leadership often necessitates a degree of separation from colleagues. Decisions about promotions, terminations, and strategic directions can create conflicts of interest or perceptions of favouritism if leaders maintain too close a relationship with those they lead. This professional distance, while necessary for maintaining objectivity and fairness, can contribute to feelings of isolation.

Consider a scenario where a leader must make a tough decision about restructuring a department, which may involve letting go of long-time colleagues or friends. The emotional burden of such decisions can be profound, and the need to remain impartial can prevent leaders from seeking solace or sharing their struggles with those directly affected. This self-imposed distance is a protective measure, but also a source of loneliness.

The Pressure of Unshared Burdens

The adage "it's lonely at the top" rings true for many leaders. The higher one rises, the fewer peers there are who share the same level of responsibility and pressure. Leaders bear the weight of critical decisions that impact not just the organisation, but also the lives of employees and their families. This responsibility can be overwhelming, and finding others who truly understand the magnitude of these burdens can be challenging.

Take, for example, the experience of leading an organisation through a financial crisis. The decisions required during such times can be gut-wrenching, involving layoffs, budget cuts, and strategic pivots. While team members may empathise, they often do not experience the full weight of these decisions. Fellow executives or leaders in similar positions may be the only ones who can offer genuine understanding and support, but such peers are rare and often just as burdened.

Emotional Solitude

Leaders are often expected to exude confidence and decisiveness, even when they are unsure or fearful. This expectation can create an emotional wall where leaders feel they must hide their vulnerabilities to maintain their authority and inspire confidence. This facade of invulnerability can prevent them from forming genuine connections and seeking the emotional support they need.

Imagine a leader facing a significant personal challenge, such as a health issue or family crisis. The expectation to remain strong and composed at work can lead to a double burden, managing personal turmoil while projecting unwavering strength professionally. This emotional solitude can exacerbate feelings of loneliness as leaders may feel there is no safe space to express their true feelings without compromising their perceived strength.

Navigating the Isolation

Despite these challenges, there are ways for leaders to navigate and mitigate the isolation inherent in their roles. Building a support network of trusted advisers, mentors, and peers who understand the unique pressures of leadership can provide a lifeline. Engaging in leadership forums, executive coaching, and peer mentoring can offer a space for sharing experiences and gaining perspective.

Additionally, practising vulnerability with trusted team members can help bridge the gap. By acknowledging their own challenges and uncertainties, leaders can foster a culture of openness and trust, encouraging others to share their struggles. This can create a more connected and supportive organisational environment, even at the highest levels of leadership.

The Weight of Responsibility

With great power comes great responsibility, and with great responsibility comes great solitude. Leaders are tasked with making tough decisions that can impact the entire organisation. These decisions often have to be made alone, adding to the sense of isolation. As former U.S. President Harry S. Truman famously said, "The buck stops here." This sentiment encapsulates the solitary burden of ultimate accountability. Every decision, from strategic direction to daily operations, carries the weight of potential consequences that can affect many lives, amplifying the loneliness of the role.

The sense of isolation is compounded by the need to project confidence and strength, even when feeling unsure. Leaders often find themselves in the paradoxical position of needing to appear invulnerable to inspire confidence, while grappling with their own doubts and insecurities. As Eleanor Roosevelt wisely noted, "To handle yourself, use your head; to handle others, use your heart." Balancing this dual responsibility can be incredibly taxing.

Lack of Intellectual Capital

Another factor contributing to the loneliness of leadership is the lack of intellectual capital around you. Leaders often find themselves surrounded by individuals who look to them for answers and guidance but who may not challenge their thinking or provide the intellectual stimulation needed for growth. This intellectual isolation can stifle innovation and prevent leaders from seeing diverse perspectives.

Engaging with peers who can provide intellectual challenge and support is crucial. Albert Einstein's observation, "It is not that I'm so smart, but I stay with the questions much longer," underscores the value of surrounding oneself with thoughtful peers who encourage prolonged engagement with complex issues. Peer groups, industry associations, and leadership forums can provide the much-needed intellectual companionship that keeps a leader's mind sharp and engaged.

The Emotional Toll

The loneliness of leadership isn't just about intellectual isolation; it also has a profound emotional impact. Leaders often have to project confidence and strength, even when they are struggling internally. This facade can prevent them from forming genuine connections and seeking the support they need.

The Burden of Projecting Strength

Leaders are frequently expected to be pillars of strength, exuding confidence and decisiveness, regardless of the internal battles they may be facing. This expectation comes from the belief that a leader's composure is integral to maintaining team morale and stability. However, the constant need to project an image of unwavering confidence can be emotionally exhausting.

Consider a moment when a company is navigating a turbulent crisis—perhaps a financial downturn or a rapid change in market dynamics. The leader steps forward, presenting a composed and reassuring demeanor to employees, investors, and stakeholders. Yet, beneath this facade of calm lies a leader grappling with intense pressure, internal conflict, and the weight of responsibility. The need to conceal these vulnerabilities, to maintain an aura of invincibility, often comes at a great cost, straining both mental and emotional resilience.

The Facade of Invulnerability

The pressure to appear invulnerable can create an emotional barrier between leaders and their teams. This facade of invulnerability can prevent leaders from forming genuine connections and seeking the support they need. By not sharing their struggles, leaders may inadvertently isolate themselves further, reinforcing the loneliness they feel.

Consider the story of a CEO who is privately dealing with a severe health issue. To maintain the confidence of the board and the employees, the CEO may choose not to disclose their condition, continuing to work as if nothing is wrong. This decision, while intended to protect the organisation, can leave the CEO feeling isolated and unsupported, unable to seek empathy or assistance from those around them.

Internalising Doubts and Fears

Leaders often internalise their doubts and fears, believing that showing any sign of weakness could undermine their authority. This internalisation can lead to chronic stress, anxiety, and even depression. The fear of being perceived as weak can prevent leaders from seeking help, further exacerbating their emotional struggles.

For example, a manager overseeing a high-stakes project might have serious concerns about meeting deadlines and achieving targets. Despite these worries, they may feel compelled to present a confident front to their team. Internally, the constant worry and fear of failure can become overwhelming, yet the leader feels trapped by the need to maintain an image of competence and control.

The Impact on Personal Relationships

The emotional toll of leadership can extend beyond the workplace, affecting personal relationships. The stress and isolation experienced by leaders can spill over into their interactions with family and friends, often leading to strained relationships. Leaders might find it difficult to switch off from their professional responsibilities, bringing the weight of their work home with them.

Consider a leader who spends long hours at the office, constantly preoccupied with work-related challenges. This focus can lead to neglecting family time and personal relationships, creating a sense of isolation both at work and at home. The inability to share the emotional burden with loved ones can further compound feelings of loneliness.

The Loneliness of Decision-Making

Decision-making is a core aspect of leadership, often marked by isolation and emotional strain. Leaders are tasked with making tough choices—such as deciding on layoffs during financial difficulties—that carry significant consequences. These decisions, made with limited information and often without full consensus, can weigh heavily on a leader's mind. The responsibility to make such impactful choices alone can amplify feelings of loneliness and the emotional toll of leadership.

Navigating the Emotional Toll

While the emotional burden of leadership is undeniable, it is not insurmountable. Leaders can mitigate this impact by embracing vulnerability and seeking support, which are essential strategies for managing their emotional well-being in the face of difficult decisions.

The Facade of Strength

I remember a time when our company was going through a particularly rough patch. Financial pressures were mounting, and the future looked uncertain. As the leader, I felt it was my duty to remain composed and reassuring for my team. Inside, however, I was grappling with fear and doubt. This facade of strength only added to my isolation, as I felt unable to share my true feelings with anyone. The need to appear invincible can create a barrier, making it difficult to find solace or support during tough times.

An anonymous quote resonates deeply with this experience: "The loneliest people are the kindest. The saddest people smile the brightest. The most damaged people are the wisest. All because they do not wish to see anyone else suffer the way they do." This encapsulates the internal conflict of leaders who, despite their own struggles, strive to shield their teams from similar pains.

The Leadership of Batman: A Lone Warrior on the Side of Good

As a lifelong fan of Batman, I've always been captivated by his complex and solitary approach to leadership. Batman, or Bruce Wayne, is not just a superhero to me; he represents the epitome of what it means to lead with purpose, resilience, and unyielding resolve. His journey from a traumatised child to Gotham's Dark Knight is a story of profound dedication, but also of deep loneliness—a dichotomy that offers valuable lessons for any leader.

Batman's leadership is defined by his relentless pursuit of justice. Unlike other superheroes blessed with extraordinary powers, Batman relies on his intellect, physical training, and an arsenal of cutting-edge technology. His commitment to honing his skills and his strategic mindset make him a formidable force in the battle against crime. But what truly sets Batman apart is his willingness to operate from the shadows, to make the hard decisions that others shy away from, even if it means isolating himself from those he protects.

In my prologue, I mentioned how Batman's story has inspired me, and it's in his solitary path that I find the most powerful lessons. Despite his outward strength, Batman's journey is marked by an intense loneliness. His role as Gotham's protector demands sacrifices that few could endure—sacrifices that often leave him alone in his mission. This loneliness is not just a byproduct of his dedication; it is an integral part of his leadership style.

Batman's dual identity further complicates his ability to connect with others. As Bruce Wayne, he must maintain a facade of normalcy, a public persona that conceals his true mission. This separation from his true self deepens his isolation, as very few people truly know or understand the burden he carries. The necessity of keeping his identity secret means that Batman must bear the weight of his struggles alone, which is a poignant reminder of the emotional toll that leadership can exact.

One of the most striking illustrations of Batman's loneliness occurs when he takes the blame for crimes he did not commit, to preserve Harvey Dent's reputation. This act of self-sacrifice, which turns him into a fugitive, exemplifies the loneliness of his path. He is willing to be misunderstood, hunted, and reviled—all in the service of a greater good. This moment, captured in Commissioner Gordon's explanation to his son—"He's the hero Gotham deserves, but not the one it needs right now"—encapsulates the solitary burden that Batman carries as Gotham's Dark Knight.

For me, Batman's leadership is a powerful example of what it means to lead with unwavering dedication, even in the face of profound loneliness. His story teaches us that the path of leadership is often isolating, but it's a path we choose because of our commitment to a cause greater than ourselves. However, it also serves as a cautionary tale: the loneliness of leadership is real, and while it may be necessary at times, it's also important to seek connection and support to avoid being consumed by the weight of our responsibilities.

Lessons from Batman's Leadership

Batman's story offers several key lessons that resonate deeply with me as a leader and a fan:

1. **Commitment to a Cause:** Batman's unwavering dedication to justice exemplifies how deeply held convictions can drive effective leadership. His resolve is a powerful reminder of the importance of staying true to our principles, even when the path is difficult.

2. **Sacrifice and Resilience:** Batman's willingness to sacrifice his personal life for the greater good is a testament to the resilience required of true leaders. His ability to endure hardship while remaining focused on his mission is both inspiring and instructive.

3. **The Importance of Allies:** Though Batman often works alone, he recognizes the value of allies. His partnerships with other heroes, though rare, highlight the benefits of support and teamwork, even for the most independent leaders.

4. **Vulnerability and Isolation:** Batman's loneliness underscores the dangers of isolation in leadership. While his solitary approach is effective, it also highlights the importance of balance and the need for support to mitigate the emotional toll of leadership.

5. **Emotional Strength:** Batman's ability to confront his fears and channel his pain into his mission exemplifies the emotional strength that leaders must cultivate. His journey teaches us that true leadership involves facing our vulnerabilities and using them as sources of strength.

Batman's leadership is an interesting combination of strength, resilience, and profound loneliness. His unwavering commitment to justice and his willingness to operate in the shadows make him a formidable protector of Gotham. Yet, his story also serves as a poignant reminder that even the most heroic leaders are not immune to loneliness, and that true strength often lies in acknowledging and confronting one's vulnerabilities. As a fan, I find endless inspiration in Batman's journey, and as a leader, I strive to embody the same dedication, resilience, and balance in my own path.

Overcoming the Loneliness

While the loneliness of leadership is a significant challenge, it is not insurmountable. There are strategies and practices that can help leaders overcome this feeling of isolation.

Building a Support Network

One of the most effective ways to combat loneliness is by building a robust support network. This network can include mentors, peers, and trusted advisers who can provide guidance, feedback, and emotional support. Regularly engaging with this network can provide a sense of connection and reduce feelings of isolation. Peer mentoring, regular networking, and participation in leadership groups can offer leaders a platform to share experiences and find mutual support.

Seeking Professional Help

Sometimes, the loneliness of leadership can become overwhelming and may require professional help. Seeking the guidance of a coach or therapist can provide a safe space to express fears, doubts, and frustrations. These professionals can offer strategies to manage stress and build resilience. Leadership coaches can provide tailored advice and help leaders develop coping mechanisms to deal with the unique pressures of their roles.

Practising Vulnerability

Embracing vulnerability can also help leaders overcome loneliness. By sharing their struggles and admitting when they don't have all the answers, leaders can build deeper, more authentic relationships with their teams. This openness can foster a culture of trust and support within the organisation. Vulnerability shows that leaders are human, creating a more inclusive and connected work environment where employees feel empowered to share their own challenges.

Special Thanks to My Support Network

During the most challenging periods of my leadership journey, I have been fortunate to have a support network that has helped me navigate the loneliness.

- **My Wife Misha**: She has always been my biggest supporter and my wisest critic. Her unwavering belief in me and her insightful feedback have been invaluable. She listens with empathy and offers perspective, making her an essential part of my support system.

- **My Mother Bhavna**: She has always stood by me, offering unconditional love and encouragement. Her strength and resilience have been a source of inspiration, helping me stay grounded and focused during difficult times.

- **My Friend Viraj**: Though not a domain expert, Viraj has been a constant source of empathy and understanding. He has always been the colleague outside the office who listened with an open heart, providing much-needed companionship during tough times.

- **My Boss Abhishek**: Always available when I felt like giving up, Abhishek's unwavering support has been a beacon of hope. His readiness to listen and offer guidance has helped me stay the course even in the darkest moments.
- **My Colleague Chintan Mehta**: The CEO of our company, Chintan Bhai, brings fun and optimism into my life. His positive outlook and ability to find joy in the small things have been a refreshing counterbalance to the pressures of leadership.

These individuals have been my pillars, helping me bear the weight of leadership, and reminding me that even at the top, one is never truly alone.

A Personal Reflection

During one of the most challenging periods of my leadership journey, I realised the importance of acknowledging and addressing my own loneliness. I reached out to a trusted mentor, Thomas, and shared my feelings of isolation. This simple act of reaching out opened the door to a wealth of support and guidance that helped me navigate the tough times.

My mentor shared with me a piece of advice that has stayed with me: "Leadership is not about being invincible. It's about being human. It's about showing your team that it's okay to be vulnerable, to seek help, and to rely on each other."

A Poetic Reflection on Loneliness

Leadership often walks a solitary path, where strength is shown, but silence speaks. This reflection captures the quiet struggle and the search for connection:

In the stillness of the night, alone,
A leader's heart is often shown.
Beneath the weight, a silent plea,
For understanding, to be free.

The burden of choices, all their own,
In shadows deep, they feel unknown.
Yet even in the darkest hour,
They seek a hand, a source of power.

For leaders, too, need strength to share,
A trusted soul who'll always care.
In shared burdens, bonds will grow,
In trusted hearts, true strength will show.

Leadership can be a lonely journey, but it doesn't have to be. By recognising the inherent isolation that comes with the role and actively seeking connection, support, and understanding, leaders can navigate their path with resilience and strength. Let us remember that true leadership is not about standing alone at the top, but about building a community of trust and support around us.

Chapter Nine

The Impact of Power

Power is a complex and multifaceted force that can shape individuals, organisations, and societies. It has the potential to inspire, uplift, and drive progress, but it can also corrupt, oppress, and lead to destructive outcomes. In the context of leadership, the impact of power is profound, influencing decisions, behaviours, and relationships. This chapter explores the dynamics of power, its effects on leadership, and the delicate balance required to wield it responsibly.

The Nature of Power

Power can be defined as the ability to influence or control the actions of others. It manifests in various forms, from positional power derived from a role or title, to personal power stemming from charisma, expertise, or relationships. The feeling of power can be intoxicating, providing a sense of authority and control. However, it also comes with significant responsibility. This duality makes power both a potent tool for good and a potential source of harm.

The Double-Edged Sword

Power is often described as a double-edged sword because of its potential to bring about both positive and negative outcomes. The same force that can drive innovation and progress can also lead to arrogance and abuse.

The Positive Impact of Power

When used responsibly, power can be a force for good. Leaders who wield power with integrity and empathy can inspire their teams, drive positive change, and create a culture of trust and collaboration. For instance, Mahatma Gandhi's use of nonviolent resistance to challenge British rule in India demonstrated how power, when guided by ethical principles, can bring about significant social and political change. Gandhi's leadership showed that true power lies not in domination, but in the ability to inspire and mobilise people towards a common cause.

The Negative Impact of Power

Conversely, power can corrupt even the best of intentions. History is replete with examples of leaders who, intoxicated by power, became authoritarian and oppressive. The story of King Lear, Shakespeare's tragic play, illustrates how the misuse of power can lead to downfall and destruction. Lear's descent into madness and the subsequent chaos in his kingdom highlight the dangers of power unchecked by wisdom and humility. Similarly, the tale of Icarus, who flew too close to the sun despite warnings, serves as a timeless reminder of the perils of hubris, or excessive pride and self-confidence.

Stories of Power in Leadership

To understand the impact of power in leadership, let's explore some stories that illustrate its diverse effects.

The Transformative Power of Vision

Steve Jobs, co-founder of Apple Inc., is often cited as a visionary leader who used his power to transform industries and inspire innovation. Jobs' ability to articulate a compelling vision and his relentless pursuit of excellence drove Apple to unprecedented heights. His power lay not just in his position, but in his ability to inspire and mobilise people towards a common goal. However, his leadership style also had its critics who pointed to his demanding and sometimes harsh approach.

The Corrupting Influence of Absolute Power

The story of Enron's downfall is a stark reminder of how absolute power can lead to unethical behaviour and catastrophic consequences. Executives at Enron used their power to manipulate financial statements and deceive stakeholders, driven by greed and the pursuit of personal gain. The collapse of Enron not only destroyed the company but also had far-reaching impacts on employees, investors, and the broader market. This story underscores the importance of accountability and ethical leadership in preventing the abuse of power.

The Quiet Power of Empathy

Jacinda Ardern, the Prime Minister of New Zealand, exemplifies the quiet power of empathy in leadership. Her compassionate response to the Christchurch mosque shootings in 2019 demonstrated how power, when exercised with empathy and humility, can heal and unite a nation. Ardern's inclusive approach and her ability to connect with people on a personal level have made her a respected and influential leader on the global stage. Her leadership highlights the importance of emotional intelligence in wielding power effectively.

The Psychological Impact of Power

Power not only affects those who wield it but also has a profound psychological impact on individuals. Studies have shown that power can alter brain function, increasing confidence and risk-taking behaviour, while reducing empathy and consideration for others. This psychological shift can lead to a disconnect between leaders and their teams, making it essential for leaders to maintain self-awareness and humility.

The Dangers of Hubris

Hubris, or excessive pride and self-confidence, is a common pitfall for those in power. Leaders who become overly confident in their abilities may ignore feedback, take unnecessary risks, and make decisions that prioritise their interests over the well-being of their team or organisation. The Greek myth of Icarus, who flew too close to the sun despite warnings, serves as a timeless cautionary tale about the dangers of hubris. Hubris can lead to a fall from grace, illustrating the importance of balance and humility in leadership.

The Need for Self-Awareness

To mitigate the negative effects of power, leaders must cultivate self-awareness. This involves regularly reflecting on their actions, seeking feedback, and being open to learning and growth. Self-aware leaders recognise their limitations and the potential impact of their decisions on others, ensuring that power is used responsibly and ethically.

Balancing Power and Responsibility

Effective leadership requires a delicate balance between power and responsibility. Leaders must navigate the complexities of wielding power while remaining grounded in their values and committed to the greater good.

Empowering Others

One of the most powerful ways to balance power and responsibility is by empowering others. This involves delegating authority, providing opportunities for growth, and fostering a culture of collaboration and trust. By empowering their teams, leaders can create a more inclusive and dynamic organisation, where everyone feels valued and motivated.

Empowering others is not just about giving them tasks to complete; it's about entrusting them with meaningful responsibilities and supporting their development. This approach helps to distribute power more evenly within the organisation, reducing the risk of centralised power becoming corrupt or overbearing. It also encourages a sense of ownership and accountability among team members, leading to higher engagement and productivity.

In my leadership journey, I have seen the transformative effect of empowering others. For example, I once encouraged a junior team member to lead a high-stakes project. Although initially hesitant, she embraced the challenge and delivered outstanding results. This experience not only boosted her confidence but also demonstrated to the entire team that everyone had the potential to lead and succeed.

Another instance involved creating cross-functional teams where members from different departments collaborated on strategic initiatives. This not only leveraged diverse skills and perspectives but also fostered a culture of mutual respect and shared leadership. Empowering these teams to make decisions and drive projects forward resulted in innovative solutions and a more agile organisation.

Practising Servant Leadership

Servant leadership, a concept popularised by Robert K. Greenleaf, emphasises the leader's role as a servant to their team. This approach prioritises the needs of others, promoting a culture of empathy, support, and shared purpose. Servant leaders use their power to uplift and develop their team members, creating a positive and sustainable impact.

Servant leadership is about listening to your team, understanding their needs, and putting their well-being first. It requires humility and a willingness to step back and let others shine. In practice, this might mean mentoring team members, providing resources for their professional development, and recognising and celebrating their achievements.

A Personal Reflection

In my leadership journey, I have experienced the impact of power in various forms. One of the most significant lessons I have learned is the importance of humility and empathy. Early in my career, I was given a leadership role that came with significant authority. The initial feeling of power was exhilarating, but it also brought immense pressure and responsibility.

I remember a particularly challenging project where my team was struggling to meet deadlines. My initial response was to exert more control, pushing my team harder and expecting immediate results. However, this approach only led to increased stress and frustration. It was a conversation with a trusted mentor that shifted my perspective.

My mentor reminded me of the importance of empathy and understanding. "Power isn't about exerting control," he said. "It's about guiding and supporting your team, especially in tough times. True leadership is about lifting others up, not pushing them down."

Taking his advice to heart, I decided to change my approach. I called a meeting with my team, but this time, I listened more than I spoke. I encouraged everyone to share their challenges and frustrations openly. It became clear that the pressure was affecting not just productivity but also morale.

"I understand that we are under a lot of stress right now," I began. "I want you all to know that I am here to support you. Let's work together to find solutions and make this project a success. Your well-being is my priority."

This shift in approach had an immediate impact. By showing vulnerability and a willingness to collaborate, I gained my team's trust and respect. The atmosphere in the room changed from one of tension to one of solidarity and mutual support. We brainstormed together, identified obstacles, and developed a more realistic timeline. The project was completed successfully, but, more importantly, we strengthened our team bond.

The Ripple Effect of Power

The impact of power extends beyond the individual leader and their immediate team. It has a ripple effect that can influence the entire organisation, and even the broader community.

Building a Legacy

Great leaders use their power to build a lasting legacy. They focus on creating systems and cultures that will endure long after they are gone. This involves mentoring future leaders, fostering a culture of continuous improvement, and ensuring that ethical standards are upheld. By doing so, they leave a positive and lasting impact that transcends their tenure.

A Poetic Reflection of Power

Power is a profound force in leadership, capable of shaping destinies and transforming lives. As I reflect on its impact, I find that poetry offers a unique lens to explore its complexities:

In guiding hands, a force so true,
Power charts the path we pursue.
To lift, to lead with mind and heart,
In every choice, true strength imparts.

The weight of power, heavy, bold,
In stories told, lives unfold.
With wisdom, empathy, and grace,
A leader's touch leaves a lasting trace.

> *In every soul, a spark of light,*
> *To wield with care, to lead with might.*
> *For power's touch can heal or scar,*
> *Its true effects seen from afar.*
>
> *In balance held and shared with all,*
> *We rise together, or we fall.*

Closing Reflection

Power is a potent tool in the hands of a leader, capable of driving profound change and fostering growth. However, it demands careful management, self-awareness, and a steadfast commitment to ethical principles. By recognizing the true impact of power and striving to use it with integrity and compassion, leaders can build legacies that uplift and inspire. As we continue to explore the nuances of power, let us remain ever mindful of its dual potential— to create and to destroy—and commit ourselves to wielding it with wisdom and grace.

Chapter Ten

The Dual Nature of Power

A Tale of Two Powers

Power manifests in many forms, and its impact is often determined by the hands that wield it. Consider two starkly contrasting figures: Genghis Khan and Mahatma Gandhi. Both were powerful in their own right, yet their use of power led them down dramatically different paths. One became synonymous with conquest and destruction, the other with peace and liberation.

The Dark Descent: Genghis Khan

Genghis Khan's rise to power is a chilling reminder of how absolute power can corrupt absolutely. Born into a nomadic tribe in Mongolia, Genghis Khan's ambitions grew as he sought to unite the Mongol tribes and conquer vast territories. His vision, fuelled by relentless ambition and a ruthless strategy, led to the creation of one of the largest empires in history, but at the cost of countless lives and widespread destruction.

Genghis Khan's ability to inspire loyalty and instil fear allowed him to manipulate and control vast armies. His reign is a stark reminder that power, when used for personal gain and driven by conquest, can lead to unimaginable atrocities. As Lord Acton famously said, "Power tends to corrupt, and absolute power corrupts absolutely." Great men are almost always bad men.

The Path of Peace: Mahatma Gandhi

In stark contrast, Mahatma Gandhi wielded power through nonviolent resistance. Born into a relatively affluent family in India, Gandhi's journey to power was driven by his commitment to justice and equality. He led India's struggle for independence from British rule, using peaceful protests and civil disobedience as his weapons.

Gandhi's power came not from force, but from his unwavering principles and ability to inspire collective action. His leadership brought about significant social change, highlighting how power, when used ethically, can uplift and liberate. "The best way to find yourself is to lose yourself in the service of others," Gandhi once said, encapsulating his approach to power.

The Corrupting Influence of Power: Hitler and Duryodhana

The stories of Hitler and Duryodhana from the Mahabharata share a common theme: the destructive potential of unchecked ambition and misuse of power.

Hitler: The Epitome of Destructive Power

Adolf Hitler's journey from a struggling artist to the dictator of Nazi Germany is marked by ruthless ambition and a relentless quest for control. His ability to tap into the frustrations and fears of the German populace post-World War I allowed him to rise rapidly through the political ranks.

Hitler's policies and actions led to World War II and the Holocaust, showing how power, when driven by a malevolent vision, can lead to catastrophic outcomes. His story serves as a grim reminder of the need for checks and balances in leadership to prevent the abuse of power. As Plato noted, "The measure of a man is what he does with power."

Duryodhana: The Tragic Antihero

In the Mahabharata, Duryodhana's thirst for power and his inability to see beyond his own desires led to the great Kurukshetra war. Duryodhana, driven by jealousy and a sense of entitlement, refused to share power with the Pandavas, his cousins. His decisions, influenced by ego and unchecked ambition, brought about the downfall of the Kaurava dynasty.

Duryodhana's story illustrates how power, when not tempered with wisdom and compassion, can lead to one's downfall and the destruction of everything one holds dear. As the Mahabharata wisely states, "A kingdom that is gained by unrighteousness and is maintained by unrighteousness shall undoubtedly perish."

The Duality of Power: The Joker

In contemporary times, fictional characters like the Joker from Batman encapsulate the chaotic and destructive nature of power when wielded by those with malevolent intentions. The Joker's character is a stark reminder of how power can corrupt and drive individuals to wreak havoc.

The Joker: Chaos Incarnate

The Joker represents the epitome of anarchic power. Unlike traditional villains who seek control, the Joker's power lies in creating chaos and instilling fear. His actions are driven by a desire to disrupt societal norms and expose the fragility of order. "Introduce a little anarchy, upset the established order, and everything becomes chaos. I'm an agent of chaos," the Joker declares in The Dark Knight.

The Joker's philosophy highlights the terrifying potential of power in the hands of those who seek to undermine and destroy, rather than build and uplift.

The Path of Justice: Batman

In contrast to the Joker, Batman represents the responsible and ethical use of power. Bruce Wayne, the man behind the mask, uses his wealth, intellect, and physical abilities to fight injustice and protect Gotham City. Unlike those who misuse power for personal gain or to instil fear, Batman's power is directed towards safeguarding others and maintaining order.

Batman: The Guardian of Gotham

Batman's power lies in his relentless pursuit of justice. Despite facing numerous personal challenges and the temptation to use his power for revenge, he remains committed to his moral code. His actions are guided by a deep sense of responsibility and a desire to protect the innocent. Batman's story illustrates that true power is not about dominance or control, but about using one's abilities and resources to make a positive impact. His commitment to justice, and his refusal to kill even his greatest enemies, underscore the importance of ethical leadership.

The Potential for Good: Empowering Others

In contrast to the destructive use of power, there are countless examples of leaders who have used their influence to empower others, fostering environments of growth, trust, and collaboration.

Nelson Mandela: A Visionary Leader

Nelson Mandela's leadership in post-apartheid South Africa is a powerful example of how power can be used to heal and unite. After spending 27 years in prison, Mandela emerged with a commitment to reconciliation rather than revenge. His ability to empower others and build a new, inclusive nation highlights the transformative potential of power when used with integrity and empathy. "It always seems impossible until it's done," Mandela once said, reflecting his resilient spirit and visionary leadership.

The Duality of Power

Power is a force that can shape destinies, transform societies, and alter the course of history. It can be a beacon of hope and progress, or a tool of oppression and destruction. The dual nature of power is evident in the stories of those who wield it, revealing how it can uplift or corrupt based on the choices and character of the leader.

The Importance of Realisation and Self-Awareness

Power has a seductive quality that can lead even the most well-intentioned leaders astray. It is crucial to remain vigilant and self-aware, recognising the moments when one might be slipping towards the dark side of power. Realisation is the key to maintaining a balance, ensuring that power is used for the greater good rather than personal gain.

Analysing the Path

In my own journey, I have faced moments where the allure of control and recognition tempted me to stray from my principles. These instances served as wake-up calls, prompting deep reflection and a recommitment to ethical leadership. By constantly analysing my actions and motivations, I strive to use power responsibly and compassionately.

Empowering Others: A Balanced Approach to Power

One of the most effective ways to wield power ethically is by empowering others. Delegating authority, fostering collaboration, and supporting the growth of team members distribute power and prevent its concentration.

Transformative Leadership

Empowering others creates an environment where individuals feel valued and motivated. It encourages a sense of ownership and accountability, leading to higher engagement and innovation.

In my leadership journey, creating cross-functional teams where members from different departments collaborate has been transformative. This approach leverages diverse skills and perspectives, fostering mutual respect and shared leadership. Empowering these teams to make decisions has resulted in innovative solutions and a more agile organisation.

As Eleanor Roosevelt wisely stated, "To handle yourself, use your head; to handle others, use your heart."

Personal Reflections on Power

Reflecting on my own journey, I see how the dual nature of power has shaped my leadership. Moments of triumph and introspection have tested my values and integrity, revealing the complexities of wielding power.

A Transformative Experience

A pivotal moment in my career was when I was entrusted with a major project during a time of organisational upheaval. The responsibility was immense, and the pressure to deliver was overwhelming. Initially, I attempted to control every aspect, believing that my direct involvement was necessary for success. This approach only led to frustration and burnout among my team.

A turning point came during a candid conversation with a junior colleague. She expressed her concerns about the lack of trust and autonomy, and her words resonated deeply with me. I realised that my approach was stifling creativity and morale. I decided to shift my strategy, empowering my team to take ownership and make decisions.

This change not only salvaged the project but also revitalised the team's spirit. It was a powerful lesson in the importance of trust, empathy, and shared leadership.

Power and Influence

Power and influence are often intertwined in leadership, yet they are distinct concepts. Understanding how to wield influence effectively, without solely relying on positional power, can lead to more sustainable and respected leadership.

Differentiating Power and Influence

Power is often associated with the ability to enforce decisions and command obedience, typically derived from one's position or authority. Influence, on the other hand, is about shaping others' behaviours, attitudes, and decisions through persuasion, inspiration, and example.

In my career, I've encountered leaders who relied heavily on their positional power, only to find that their influence waned when they were no longer in that position. Conversely, those who mastered the art of influence often continued to inspire and lead, regardless of their official title.

Building Influence Without Positional Power

1. **Develop Expertise:** Being knowledgeable and competent in your field builds respect and influence.
2. **Build Relationships:** Cultivate strong, genuine relationships based on trust and mutual respect.
3. **Lead by Example:** Demonstrate the behaviours and work ethic you expect from others.
4. **Communicate Effectively:** Articulate your vision and ideas clearly and compellingly.
5. **Empower Others:** Give team members the autonomy and resources they need to succeed, which fosters loyalty and trust.

Redemption and Responsibility

Despite its potential for harm, power also holds the potential for redemption. Leaders who recognise their mistakes, seek to learn and grow, and use their power to make amends, can transform their impact and legacy.

The Journey of Redemption

I recall a leader I once admired, who initially succumbed to the temptations of power. His need for control and recognition led to significant mistakes and the loss of trust. However, he had the humility to acknowledge his flaws and the courage to change. He embarked on a journey of redemption, focusing on rebuilding trust, empowering others, and prioritising the greater good over personal gain. His story is a great reminder of the possibility of redemption and the transformative power of humility and integrity.

The Complexity of Power: A Question of Balance

Power is not inherently good or evil; it is the intent and actions of those who wield it that determine its impact. Understanding this duality is crucial for any leader. It requires a commitment to self-awareness, humility, and a focus on using power for the greater good.

As we continue this journey, let us embrace the complexities of power, acknowledging its potential for both creation and destruction. Let us strive to wield it responsibly and ethically, always mindful of its profound impact on our lives and those we lead. As Spider-Man famously said, "With great power comes great responsibility."

A Strange Close: The Ongoing Quest for Ethical Power

Power remains an enigmatic force, constantly challenging us to question our motives and actions. As leaders, it is our duty to reflect on our use of power, to seek balance, and to strive for a legacy that uplifts rather than oppresses. The journey is ongoing, filled with moments of doubt and realisation.

In the end, the true measure of power lies not in its possession, but in its application. How we choose to use our power defines us and shapes the world around us. As you ponder these reflections, ask yourself: How will you wield your power? What legacy will you leave behind?

A Poetic Reflection on the Dual Nature of Power

Power, in its duality, shapes both the light and the shadow of leadership. As I reflect on its influence, poetry offers a profound way to explore its complexities:

In hands that hold both dark and light,
Power leaves its lasting sight.
To lift, to lead with mind and heart,
In every choice, true strength does start.

The siren's call, the shadow's snare,
In power's grip, we must beware.
Yet deep within each leader's core,
The seeds of virtue we must restore.

For power's touch can mend or break,
Its true weight in choices we make.
With balance kept and wisdom clear,
We wield our power, year by year.

To serve, to guide with humble grace,
In power's mirror, our truth we trace.

As we explore the intricate nature of power, let us remain vigilant and introspective, always questioning how we use our influence.

The path to understanding power is unending, but through this journey, we discover our true strength and purpose. It is in the balance of power, guided by wisdom and humility, that we find our greatest potential to lead for the betterment of all.

Chapter Eleven

Styles of Leadership: Adapting to Thrive

Leadership is not a one-size-fits-all concept. Different situations, teams, and goals require different leadership styles. The ability to adapt one's leadership style to meet the needs of the moment is a hallmark of effective leadership. In this chapter, we will explore various styles of leadership, their applications, and real-life examples that illustrate their impact.

Understanding Leadership Styles

There are several well-recognised leadership styles, each with its strengths and weaknesses. Understanding these styles and knowing when to apply them can significantly enhance a leader's effectiveness.

Transformational Leadership

Characteristics:

- Inspires and motivates through a shared vision.
- Encourages innovation and creativity.

- Focuses on the growth and development of team members.
- Builds strong relationships and fosters a positive work culture.

A Transformational Leader: Steve Jobs

Steve Jobs is often cited as a quintessential transformational leader. His ability to articulate a compelling vision for Apple and his relentless drive for innovation inspired his team to create groundbreaking products like the iPhone and iPad. Jobs' leadership transformed Apple into one of the most valuable companies in the world.

Reference: "The Innovator's Dilemma" by Clayton Christensen

Transactional Leadership

Characteristics:

- Sets clear goals and expectations.
- Uses rewards and punishments to motivate.
- Emphasises efficiency and standardisation.
- Monitors performance closely.

A Transactional Leader: Bill Gates

Bill Gates, during his time at Microsoft, demonstrated transactional leadership. He set clear goals, provided rewards for success, and enforced consequences for failure. This approach helped Microsoft achieve significant market dominance in the software industry.

Reference: "Drive: The Surprising Truth About What Motivates Us" by Daniel H. Pink.

Servant Leadership

Characteristics:

- Prioritises the needs and well-being of team members.
- Practices empathy and active listening.
- Focuses on the growth and development of others.
- Leads by example and fosters a collaborative environment.

Real-Life Example: Herb Kelleher

Herb Kelleher, the co-founder of Southwest Airlines, is a well-known servant leader. He fostered a culture of mutual respect and trust, putting employees first, which, in turn, led to exceptional customer service and business success.
Reference: "The Servant as Leader" by Robert K. Greenleaf.

Authoritative Leadership

Characteristics:

- Sets a clear vision and direction.
- Makes decisions independently.
- Expects compliance from team members.
- Provides strong, directive leadership.

Real-Life Example: Elon Musk

Elon Musk's leadership style at Tesla and SpaceX is often described as authoritative. He sets ambitious goals and has a clear vision for the future. His decisive, and sometimes uncompromising, approach has driven significant advancements in electric vehicles and space exploration.

Reference: "Elon Musk: Tesla, SpaceX, and the Quest for a Fantastic Future" by Ashlee Vance.

Laissez-Faire Leadership

Characteristics:

- Takes a hands-off approach.
- Provides team members with autonomy.
- Encourages independence and self-motivation.
- Intervenes only when necessary.

Real-Life Example: Warren Buffett

Warren Buffett, the CEO of Berkshire Hathaway, employs a laissez-faire leadership style. He trusts his managers to run their businesses independently, providing them with the autonomy to make decisions and drive performance.

Reference: "The Warren Buffett Way," by Robert G. Hagstrom.

Visionary Leadership

Visionary leadership is about creating and communicating a compelling vision for the future that inspires and motivates others. Visionary leaders are not just dreamers; they are strategic thinkers who can turn their vision into reality.

The Essence of Visionary Leadership

Visionary leaders possess several key traits:

1. **Clear Vision:** They have a well-defined and compelling vision of what they want to achieve.
2. **Inspirational Communication:** They can effectively communicate their vision and inspire others to share it.

3. **Strategic Thinking:** They can devise strategies to turn their vision into actionable plans.
4. **Resilience:** They persist through challenges and remain committed to their vision.
5. **Adaptability:** They are flexible and can adjust their strategies in response to changing circumstances.

The Role of Vision in Leadership

A clear vision provides direction and purpose. It aligns the efforts of the team, fosters a sense of unity, and motivates individuals to work towards a common goal. Visionary leadership can transform organisations and drive significant progress.

Case Study: Elon Musk

Elon Musk is renowned for his visionary leadership. His vision for sustainable energy and space exploration has driven the success of companies like Tesla and SpaceX. Musk's ability to articulate his vision and rally people behind it has been a key factor in achieving groundbreaking innovations.

Musk's leadership style is characterised by his relentless pursuit of ambitious goals. He inspires his teams to push the boundaries of what is possible, fostering a culture of innovation and resilience.

Techniques for Developing and Communicating a Vision

1. **Identify Core Values:** Understand what is most important to you and your organisation.
2. **Set Long-Term Goals:** Define where you want to be in the future.

3. **Communicate Clearly:** Use compelling narratives to share your vision with others.
4. **Involve Your Team:** Encourage input and buy-in from your team members.
5. **Lead by Example:** Demonstrate commitment to your vision through your actions.

Personal Experiences: Crafting and Communicating Vision

In one of my leadership roles, I was tasked with turning around a struggling department. I began by defining a clear vision for revitalising our operations and communicated this vision through regular team meetings and updates. By involving the team in the planning process and demonstrating my commitment to our goals, we were able to transform the department's performance and morale.

One memorable instance was when we faced a significant budget cut. Instead of panicking, I gathered the team, and together, we redefined our vision, focusing on efficiency and innovation. This collaborative approach not only helped us overcome the financial challenge but also strengthened our sense of unity and purpose.

Conclusion: The Power of Visionary Leadership

Visionary leadership is about seeing beyond the present and inspiring others to work towards a better future. It involves strategic thinking, effective communication, and unwavering commitment. By developing and communicating a clear vision, leaders can drive significant progress and create a lasting impact.

Adapting Leadership Styles to Situations

Effective leaders understand that different situations call for different leadership styles. Adapting one's approach based on the context can lead to better outcomes and more resilient teams.

Crisis Situations

In times of crisis, an authoritative leadership style may be necessary to make quick decisions and provide clear direction. However, as the situation stabilises, transitioning to a more collaborative or transformational style can help rebuild trust and morale.

Example: Winston Churchill

During World War II, Winston Churchill demonstrated authoritative leadership, making decisive and often tough decisions to guide Britain through the conflict. His clear vision and unwavering resolve were crucial in maintaining national morale and achieving victory.

Reference: "Churchill: Walking with Destiny" by Andrew Roberts.

Innovation and Change

During periods of innovation and change, transformational leadership can inspire and motivate teams to embrace new ideas and drive progress. Leaders must create a vision that excites and engages their team, fostering a culture of creativity and continuous improvement.

Example: Reed Hastings

Reed Hastings, co-founder and CEO of Netflix, used transformational leadership to pivot the company from a DVD rental service to a streaming giant, continuously pushing for innovation and adaptation in a rapidly changing industry.

Reference: "No Rules Rules: Netflix and the Culture of Reinvention" by Reed Hastings and Erin Meyer.

Routine Operations

In more stable and routine environments, a transactional leadership style can ensure efficiency and consistency. Setting clear expectations, monitoring performance, and providing feedback are crucial in such contexts.

Example: Jeff Bezos

Jeff Bezos, during his tenure at Amazon, combined transactional leadership with a relentless focus on operational efficiency, leading to the company's dominance in e-commerce and cloud computing.

Reference: "The Everything Store: Jeff Bezos and the Age of Amazon" by Brad Stone.

Sustainability Through Adaptive Leadership

Adaptability in leadership not only ensures success in varying situations, but also fosters sustainability. Leaders who can pivot their style to meet the demands of their environment can create lasting impacts and build resilient organisations.

Story: Satya Nadella's Leadership at Microsoft

When Satya Nadella took over as CEO of Microsoft, the company was seen as lagging behind in innovation, especially in the cloud computing space. Nadella's leadership brought a significant cultural shift, focusing on empathy, collaboration, and a growth mindset. Initially adopting a transformational leadership style, he inspired a shared vision and fostered a culture of learning and innovation.

Nadella also demonstrated servant leadership by prioritising employee development and well-being, which revitalised

Microsoft's corporate culture. By integrating these adaptive leadership styles, he led Microsoft to regain its position as a technology leader, driving growth in cloud services and AI.

Reference: "Hit Refresh: The Quest to Rediscover Microsoft's Soul and Imagine a Better Future for Everyone" by Satya Nadella.

Personal Reflections on Leadership Adaptation

Throughout my career, I have found that adapting my leadership style to the needs of the moment has been critical to my success. There were times when I had to be authoritative, making tough decisions quickly. At other times, being a servant leader, focusing on the growth and well-being of my team, was the key to fostering a collaborative and motivated environment.

A Transformative Experience

A pivotal moment came when I was leading a major project that required innovation and collaboration. Initially, I took a transactional approach, setting clear goals and monitoring progress closely. However, I soon realised that my team needed inspiration and freedom to explore new ideas. Shifting to a transformational leadership style, I shared a compelling vision and encouraged creativity. This change not only enhanced the project's success, but also empowered my team to reach their full potential.

Conclusion: The Art of Adapting to Thrive

Leadership is an evolving art that requires constant adaptation. The ability to switch between different styles, based on the situation and the needs of the team, is a crucial skill for any leader. By understanding and mastering various leadership styles, leaders can thrive in diverse environments, drive their teams to success, and leave a lasting positive impact.

References

Christensen, Clayton. "The Innovator's Dilemma."

Pink, Daniel H. "Drive: The Surprising Truth About What Motivates Us."

Greenleaf, Robert K. "The Servant as Leader."

Vance, Ashlee. "Elon Musk: Tesla, SpaceX, and the Quest for a Fantastic Future."

Hagstrom, Robert G. "The Warren Buffett Way."

Roberts, Andrew. "Churchill: Walking with Destiny."

Hastings, Reed, and Meyer, Erin. "No Rules Rules: Netflix and the Culture of Reinvention."

Stone, Brad. "The Everything Store: Jeff Bezos and the Age of Amazon."

Nadella, Satya. "Hit Refresh: The Quest to Rediscover Microsoft's Soul and Imagine a Better Future for Everyone."

By delving into the various leadership styles and understanding their applications, this chapter aims to provide leaders with the tools they need to adapt and thrive in any situation. The stories and examples serve as a guide, illustrating the impact of different styles and the importance of flexibility in leadership.

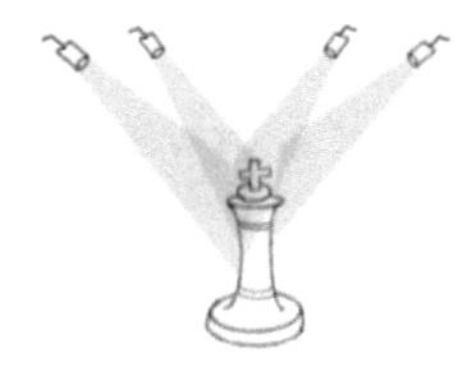

Chapter Twelve

Confessions of a Leader

In this chapter, we delve into the deepest, often unspoken truths about power and leadership through the revelations and confessions of those who have wielded it. These real-life stories and insights from leaders, politicians, actors, and even fictional characters offer a profound understanding of the dual nature of power.

Elon Musk

Elon Musk, CEO of Tesla and SpaceX, is known for his ambitious vision and relentless drive. However, he has openly discussed the immense stress and personal sacrifices involved in his journey. "The reality is great highs, terrible lows, and unrelenting stress. Don't think people want to hear about the last two," Musk admitted. This vulnerability highlights the human side of his extraordinary achievements and the toll that pursuing such a vision can take. While the highs are celebrated, Musk's confession reminds us that the journey to the top is often paved with significant challenges.

Jeff Bezos

Jeff Bezos, the founder of Amazon, has often spoken about the challenges of leadership. He once confessed, "I've made billions of dollars of failures at Amazon.com. Literally billions." Bezos's admission of failure and learning from those experiences illustrates the resilience required to sustain power and success in the long-term. It's a reminder that even the most successful leaders face setbacks and must learn to navigate them to achieve lasting success.

Angela Merkel

Angela Merkel, former Chancellor of Germany, known for her pragmatic and steady leadership, has spoken about the pressures of holding office. She once shared, "Power is fascinating and dangerous. It requires a constant effort to remain grounded and connected to the people you serve." Merkel's confession underscores the delicate balance required to wield power responsibly while staying true to one's values. Her journey highlights the importance of maintaining a connection to the people you lead, ensuring that power is used for the collective good.

Richard Nixon

Richard Nixon, the 37th President of the United States, once said in a moment of reflection, "I gave them a sword, and they stuck it in, and they twisted it with relish." His involvement in the Watergate scandal, driven by a desperate desire to maintain power, led to his resignation and forever tainted his legacy. Nixon's confession highlights how power can drive individuals to ethical breaches and irreversible actions, serving as a cautionary tale of the dangers of unchecked ambition.

Oprah Winfrey

Oprah Winfrey, a beacon of empowerment and leadership, once shared, "I had no idea that being your authentic self could make me as rich as I've become. If I had, I'd have done it a lot earlier." Oprah's journey from poverty to becoming one of the most powerful media moguls illustrates the positive use of power. Yet, she also acknowledges the pressures and responsibilities that come with it, often leading to moments of self-doubt and reflection. Her story underscores the importance of authenticity in leadership.

Steve Jobs

Steve Jobs, the visionary co-founder of Apple, famously admitted, "I'm convinced that about half of what separates successful entrepreneurs from the non-successful ones is pure perseverance." Jobs' relentless pursuit of innovation often led to strained relationships and high-pressure environments. His confession underscores the fine line between visionary leadership and the potential for creating a toxic work culture. It's a reminder that perseverance must be balanced with empathy and understanding.

Nelson Mandela

Nelson Mandela, a symbol of resilience and moral leadership, reflected on his long struggle against apartheid, saying, "I learned that courage was not the absence of fear, but the triumph over it. The brave man is not he who does not feel afraid, but he who conquers that fear." Mandela's use of power for societal good contrasts sharply with those who use it for personal gain, highlighting the profound impact of ethical leadership.

Mahatma Gandhi

Mahatma Gandhi, a global symbol of nonviolent resistance, confessed his inner conflicts and imperfections. He wrote, "I claim to be no more than an average man with below-average capabilities. I have not the shadow of a doubt that any man or woman can achieve what I have if he or she would make the same effort and cultivate the same hope and faith." Gandhi's humility and self-awareness underline the humanity behind his towering legacy.

Theodore Roosevelt

Theodore Roosevelt, the 26th President of the United States, once said, "I have always been afraid of a man who knew too much." Roosevelt's recognition of the limits of knowledge and the importance of continuous learning reflects a deep understanding of the responsibilities of power.

Ruth Bader Ginsburg

Ruth Bader Ginsburg, the late Supreme Court Justice, shared insights into the pressures of her role. "Reacting in anger or annoyance will not advance one's ability to persuade," she advised. Ginsburg's confession about maintaining composure and effectiveness in the face of challenges highlights the emotional discipline required in leadership.

Fictional Character – Michael Corleone (The Godfather)

Michael Corleone, the protagonist of "The Godfather,", provides a fictional yet poignant confession about power. He states, "My father taught me many things here — he taught me in this room. He taught me — keep your friends close, but your enemies closer." Michael's journey from a reluctant family member to a ruthless mafia boss exemplifies how power can corrupt and transform even the most well-intentioned individuals.

The Strange Things Power Makes Us Do

Throughout history, power has driven people to do strange, sometimes unthinkable things. These confessions illustrate how the allure of power can lead to actions that defy ethical and moral boundaries.

The Corporate Leader's Dilemma

A prominent CEO once confessed that the higher he climbed the corporate ladder, the lonelier he felt. The power he amassed alienated him from his peers and friends. He admitted to making decisions that compromised his values to maintain his position, leading to a deep sense of regret and isolation. "I thought I could use my position to make a difference, but in the end, it consumed me. I became someone I no longer recognised," he lamented. This confession underscores the importance of staying true to one's values and the dangers of letting power isolate you.

The Political Leader's Confession

A politician I admired for his integrity confessed that the demands of holding office forced him to make alliances with individuals he once considered adversaries. The compromises he made eroded his sense of self, and he often wondered if the power was worth the personal cost. "In politics, the lines between right and wrong blur. You start with ideals, but the reality of maintaining power forces you to adapt in ways you never imagined," he revealed. His story highlights the ethical dilemmas faced by those in power and the importance of maintaining one's moral compass.

My Confessions: A Leader's Journey

Reflecting on these powerful confessions from historical and contemporary figures, I find parallels in my own journey. Born into a wealthy family with strong values and expectations, my path was shaped by both privilege and adversity. Despite excelling in academics and achieving professional success, I often grappled with the true nature of power and its impact on my life and those around me.

The Weight of Responsibility

As a leader, the weight of responsibility is an ever-present force, shaping decisions, actions, and the very essence of who you are. This burden can be inspiring and crushing, a dual-edged sword that demands constant balancing. For me, this journey was deeply personal and often conflicted, as the expectations placed upon me led to a profound internal struggle.

From a young age, I was aware of the high expectations set by my family. Born into wealth, my upbringing was steeped in values of hard work, integrity and excellence. My mother's relentless drive and high standards became the foundation of my own ambitions. Excelling in academics and later in my professional life, I found myself constantly wearing a mask. This mask represented confidence, decisiveness and unwavering strength. I felt responsible for maintaining this facade, fearing that any sign of vulnerability would undermine my authority and the trust my team placed in me.

The mask became a part of my identity, a shield that protected me from the pressures and scrutiny of leadership. However, it also isolated me, making it difficult to connect authentically with others and to share my true self. The weight of responsibility turned into a prison of my own making, where vulnerability was seen as a weakness, rather than strength.

The Turning Point

The turning point came during a particularly challenging period at work. The pressure was immense, and I found myself at a breaking point. One evening, a senior colleague approached me and said, "Are you okay? Can I help you?" As we talked, she expressed her own fears and doubts, and in that moment, I realised that I was not alone in feeling overwhelmed.

Taking a deep breath, I decided to share my own struggles with her. I admitted my fears of failure, the pressure to always have the answers, and the toll it was taking on me. To my surprise, her response was one of empathy and support. She thanked me for being honest and said it made her feel more connected and understood.

This interaction was a revelation. I realised that vulnerability was not a weakness, but a bridge that connected me to my team. By showing my true self, I could foster a deeper sense of trust and collaboration.

"Vulnerability is the birthplace of innovation, creativity, and change," – Brené Brown.

From that moment on, I made a conscious effort to embrace vulnerability in my leadership. I started sharing more openly with my team, acknowledging when I didn't have all the answers and seeking their input and collaboration. This shift transformed our dynamic, creating a culture of mutual support and openness. My team began to feel more empowered and engaged, knowing that their leader was not infallible, but human, just like them. By embracing my vulnerabilities, I allowed others to embrace theirs, fostering an environment of authenticity and trust.

I also began to prioritise self-care and emotional well-being. I sought mentorship from leaders who valued empathy and vulnerability, learning from their experiences and applying those lessons in my own journey. These changes not only improved my leadership, but also my personal relationships, as I became more present and authentic in all aspects of my life.

"It is not the mountain we conquer, but ourselves." – Sir Edmund Hillary

The Power of Authentic Leadership

Embracing vulnerability allowed me to shed the mask and lead with authenticity. It taught me that true strength lies in acknowledging our imperfections and seeking connection through shared experiences. This approach not only made me a better leader, but also enriched my life in countless ways.

The *Daily* Battle of Self-Reflection

In day-to-day conversations, I often find myself at loggerheads with myself, where disappointment takes over due to the behaviour of others. It's a constant struggle to balance expectations and reality, to maintain empathy while addressing challenges, and to navigate the myriad emotions that come with leadership. This internal conflict is a significant part of my journey as a leader, and it has taught me valuable lessons about resilience and self-awareness.

I also find myself in constant dialogue with other leaders I work with. These leaders come with differing styles – some are authoritative and get their work done through sheer force of will, while others are more collaborative and inclusive. This diversity in leadership approaches often leads to intense discussions and debates. It's in these moments that I realise the importance of understanding and respecting different perspectives, even when they conflict with my own.

The battle of self-reflection is an everyday affair. There are moments when I question my decisions, my approach, and even my core values. These conflicting thoughts are part of the process of growth and learning. I've come to understand that there is no perfect leadership style. Each day brings new challenges and opportunities to learn something new.

Every leader has their unique way of handling situations, and what works for one may not work for another. The key is to remain flexible and open-minded, to adapt and evolve continuously. This realisation has helped me embrace the uncertainty and complexity of leadership. It has allowed me to see each day as a chance to improve and to make a positive impact.

Reflecting on these daily battles, I understand that leadership is not about having all the answers or always being right. It's about being honest with oneself, learning from mistakes, and striving to be better. It's about finding a balance between firmness and compassion, between guiding and listening, and between leading and learning.

This section of my confessions is a testament to the ongoing journey of self-discovery and growth. It's a reminder that leadership is a dynamic and evolving process, filled with challenges and triumphs, conflicts, and resolutions. Each day is an opportunity to learn, to reflect, and to become a better leader.

Lord Ram: The Epitome of Leadership and Power

In the vast tapestry of leadership archetypes, Lord Ram stands as an epitome of righteousness, compassion, and unwavering duty. Revered not just as a deity, but as an ideal leader, his life and actions offer timeless lessons on the ethical use of power and the importance of integrity.

The Virtues of Lord Ram

Lord Ram's leadership was characterised by his deep sense of justice, humility, and commitment to his people. Unlike many leaders who seek power for personal gain, Lord Ram viewed his role as a sacred duty, a responsibility to uphold dharma (righteousness), and ensure the well-being of his kingdom.

One of the most striking aspects of Lord Ram's leadership was his adherence to truth and justice, even when it caused personal pain. When he was unjustly exiled from his kingdom for fourteen years, he accepted the decree without resentment. This act of obedience to his father's promise demonstrated his respect for family honour and the rule of law, setting a powerful example for his followers.

> "Rama's heart was pure, and his soul was noble. He was the personification of virtue and righteousness."
>
> –Tulsidas, Ramcharitmanas

Compassionate Leadership

Lord Ram's compassion was evident in how he treated everyone with respect and kindness, regardless of their status. His interactions with Hanuman, Sugriva, and even the vanaras (monkey warriors) of Kishkindha, reflect his ability to see and nurture potential in others, regardless of their origins. He inspired loyalty not through fear, but through genuine care and respect.

The Battle Against Ravana

The epic battle against Ravana, the demon king of Lanka, showcases Lord Ram's strategic acumen and moral fortitude. Despite the immense personal stakes, he fought with honour, adhering to the principles of warfare. His decision to offer Ravana multiple chances to surrender, and his respect for Ravana's bravery and abilities, even as an adversary, highlight his fairness and magnanimity.

Balancing Power with Humility

Perhaps the most remarkable aspect of Lord Ram's leadership is his humility. Despite his divine status, he lived and acted as a mortal, accepting the challenges and pains of human life. This humility allowed him to connect deeply with his subjects, earning their love and respect, not just as a king, but as a moral guide and protector.

Lord Ram's rule, often referred to as Ram Rajya, is remembered as a time of peace, prosperity, and justice. It serves as an ideal that leaders across generations strive to emulate, a society where the ruler is wise and compassionate, and where justice and virtue prevail.

Personal Reflection

I have always believed that you see in God the qualities that attract you. For me, Lord Ram embodies the qualities I aspire to have as a leader: integrity, compassion, humility, and unwavering commitment to duty. His life teaches that true power lies in serving others and upholding moral values, even in the face of great adversity.

"A leader is one who knows the way, goes the way, and shows the way." – John C. Maxwell

The Challenge of Changing People

One of the most challenging aspects of leadership was dealing with people who misused their power. I often found myself disappointed and hurt by those who prioritised their ambitions over ethical conduct. The question of whether people can truly change is one that I grappled with frequently.

The Power of Influence

While it is difficult to change people, leaders have the power to influence. By setting an example, fostering a culture of integrity, and holding others accountable, it is possible to inspire positive change. However, this is an ongoing process that requires patience and resilience.

> "The greatest leader is not necessarily the one who does the greatest things. He is the one who gets the people to do the greatest things."
>
> –Ronald Reagan

The Duality of Power

As I reflect on these confessions, the duality of power and the complexities of leadership, I realise that the journey is far from over. The quest for understanding and wielding power ethically is ongoing. It is a path filled with contradictions, challenges, and profound revelations.

In the end, the true measure of a leader is not just in their achievements, but in their ability to navigate the intricate dance between power and humility, ambition, and integrity. As you ponder these reflections, ask yourself: What does power mean to you? How will you wield it?

> **A Poetic Reflection on Power**
>
> Reflecting on the dual nature of power, I find solace and insight in poetry. Here's a piece that captures the essence of power in leadership:
>
> *In the shadows and the light,*
> *Power sways both day and night.*
> *A tool for good, a weapon of might,*
> *In every heart, a constant fight.*
>
> *To lead with grace, to guide with care,*
> *A leader's burden, a heavy wear.*
> *In every choice, a path we chart,*
> *The true power lies within the heart.*

Closing Thoughts

The journey of leadership is a continuous one, marked by triumphs and trials, successes, and failures. It is a journey that requires constant reflection, humility, and a willingness to grow and adapt. As leaders, we must embrace the dual nature of power, understanding that it can be a force for good or a source of destruction. By leading with integrity, empathy, and authenticity, we can navigate this complex landscape and inspire others to do the same.

"The woods are lovely, dark and deep,

But I have promises to keep,

And miles to go before I sleep,

And miles to go before I sleep." –Robert Frost

These confessions reveal the nuanced, often conflicting nature of power. It is a force that can elevate and destroy, inspire, and corrupt. As we continue this exploration, let us embrace the complexities of leadership, striving always to use our power for the greater good.

like that: taking on significant responsibilities and using the power that comes with it to create positive outcomes.

Power Amplifies Responsibility

Fast forward to my early career as an accountant, suddenly thrust into a leadership role at 24. Imagine joining a company that was growing but lacked processes, vision, and motivation. I was responsible for not just steering the company towards profitability, but also building a culture of trust and integrity.

In the early days, I was seen as merely a "numbers guy." My colleagues doubted my ability to inspire. But I drew from my childhood experiences of fitting into the world, learning the power of empathy and connection. These skills were crucial in gaining my team's trust and steering the company forward.

One of the most vivid examples of balancing power and responsibility was when we had to decide on a massive investment. Picture this: you have the power to decide the future of the company, but with that power comes the responsibility for your team's livelihood. The sleepless nights spent analysing data weren't just about numbers, but about the potential impact on my team. The decision led to unprecedented growth, proving that when power is exercised with a sense of responsibility, it can mobilise and elevate an entire organisation.

The Ethical Compass

Navigating the balance also means staying true to one's ethical compass. Imagine being offered a lucrative deal that requires compromising your ethical standards. The pressure to deliver results is immense, but you know that compromising your values will set a dangerous precedent.

Choosing the path of integrity, even at the cost of short-term gains, reinforced a culture of trust within the organisation. True power in leadership comes not from dominating others, but from inspiring trust and confidence.

Empowerment Through Delegation

Another lesson is the art of delegation. Early in my leadership journey, I was overwhelmed, trying to control every aspect of the business. This micromanagement stemmed from a misplaced sense of responsibility, believing that I had to bear the burden alone.

Think of your favourite sports team. The coach can't play every position; they need to trust their players. Similarly, by delegating tasks and trusting my team, I fostered a sense of ownership and accountability. This shift led to a more dynamic and resilient organisation, capable of tackling challenges collectively.

Lessons from Failure

Leadership isn't devoid of failures. Picture a project falling apart due to unforeseen market changes. As the leader, the responsibility of this failure fell squarely on me. Instead of deflecting blame, I took full responsibility. This transparency was crucial in maintaining the team's morale and trust.

Reflecting on failures, learning from them, and moving forward with renewed determination is vital. It reinforces that power in leadership also entails the courage to own up to failures and the resilience to bounce back stronger.

The Dual Nature of Power

Leadership is a continual act of balancing power and responsibility. Power, when exercised responsibly, can lead to remarkable achievements and foster a culture of trust and integrity. Conversely, power without accountability can quickly erode the very foundation of leadership.

A Contemporary Example of Balance

One of the best examples of balancing power and responsibility in recent times is Tim Cook, CEO of Apple. When he took over from Steve Jobs, he inherited immense power but also the significant responsibility of leading one of the world's most influential companies. Cook's leadership has been marked by a commitment to privacy, sustainability, and human rights. He has leveraged Apple's power, not just for profit, but to drive social change, showcasing that true leadership lies in using power responsibly to make a positive impact.

Think about superheroes. Batman's power isn't just his physical strength or gadgets; it's his unwavering sense of responsibility to protect Gotham. Similarly, as leaders, our power lies not in authority, but in our commitment to our team's well-being and success.

As I reflect on my journey, from a young, uncertain boy to a leader in a global business landscape, the balance between power and responsibility remains the cornerstone of my leadership philosophy. This balance transforms power from a tool of authority into a force for positive change, guiding teams toward shared goals and collective success.

Leadership, in its truest form, isn't about standing above others, but standing with them, bearing the weight of responsibility with integrity, and using power to uplift and empower. This delicate balance is the essence of effective leadership and the key to navigating the intricate dance of power and responsibility.

The Journey of Empowering Leadership

My own journey has been marked by a series of transformative experiences that underscore the importance of balancing power with responsibility. Early in my career, I faced numerous challenges that tested my leadership and ethical values.

One such experience involved a high-stakes project that required significant investment and carried substantial risk. The power to make this decision was mine, but so was the responsibility for its potential impact on the company and its employees. After careful consideration and extensive consultation with my team, I decided to proceed with the investment. The project succeeded beyond expectations, leading to substantial growth for the company. This success reinforced the lesson that power, when wielded responsibly and with a sense of duty, can lead to extraordinary outcomes.

Reflecting on Personal Growth

As I look back on these experiences, I realise that the most significant growth came not from the successes, but from the failures and challenges. Each failure was an opportunity to learn, to reflect, and to improve. It was during these times that the true balance of power and responsibility became evident.

One particularly challenging period involved a strategic misstep that resulted in significant financial losses. Accepting responsibility for the failure was difficult, but it was also necessary for maintaining the trust and respect of my team. By owning up to the mistake and working collaboratively to rectify it, we emerged stronger and more resilient. This experience underscored the importance of humility and accountability in leadership.

The Role of Empathy and Connection

Throughout my leadership journey, empathy and connection have been central to balancing power and responsibility. Understanding the needs, concerns, and aspirations of my team has enabled me to make more informed and compassionate decisions. It has also fostered a culture of mutual respect and trust.

One memorable example involved a team member who was struggling with personal issues that affected his performance. Instead of reprimanding him, I took the time to understand his situation and offer support. This empathy not only helped him overcome his challenges but also strengthened his loyalty and commitment to the team. This experience highlighted that true leadership is not about exerting control, but about empowering and uplifting others.

The Legacy of Ethical Leadership

As I continue to navigate the complexities of leadership, I am constantly reminded of the delicate balance between power and responsibility. The lessons learned from historical figures, contemporary leaders, and my own experiences have shaped my understanding of ethical leadership.

The legacy of ethical leadership lies in its ability to inspire and empower future generations. By upholding values of integrity, empathy, and accountability, leaders can create a positive and lasting impact on their organisations and society. This legacy is not just measured by achievements, but by the trust, respect, and inspiration that leaders leave behind.

A Poetic Reflection on Leadership

As I contemplate the challenge of balancing power with responsibility, poetry offers both insight and comfort. Here's a piece that captures the essence of ethical leadership:

In the dance of power, a leader's grace,
Lies not in might, but in the heart's embrace.
To guide with wisdom, to lead with care,
In every choice, a burden we bear.

The path is steep, the journey long,
With every step, a guiding song.
For in the balance of power and trust,
We find our purpose, noble and just.

To lead with honor, to stand with pride,
In the hearts of those we lift and guide.
For true power lies not in command,
But in the strength of a helping hand.

Leadership is a delicate balance of power and responsibility. It requires a commitment to ethical values, a willingness to learn from failures, and an unwavering dedication to the well-being of others. As we continue this journey, let us strive to wield our power responsibly and to inspire others with our integrity and compassion. The true measure of a leader lies not in their authority, but in their ability to uplift and empower those they lead.

Chapter Fourteen

Abuse of Power - The Dark Path

Power, in its most benevolent form, can elevate and inspire. But, in its most malevolent form, it can destroy, kill, and humiliate. This chapter delves into the shadowy abyss of power's potential for abuse, where ambition turns toxic, and the consequences are devastating.

The Descent into Darkness

Imagine a leader who starts with the best intentions. They rise through the ranks, their ambition fuelled by a desire to make a difference. But as their power grows, so does their ego. They begin to see themselves as invincible, above the rules that govern others. The lines between right and wrong blur, and their moral compass shatters. What follows is a descent into darkness.

Consider the story of a once-beloved CEO. In the early days, he was hailed as a visionary, a beacon of innovation. But with power came a sense of entitlement. He began to exploit his position, using company funds for personal luxuries, manipulating financial reports to inflate profits, and silencing anyone who dared to question his authority. Employees who once admired him now feared him. The company's culture of trust and collaboration eroded, replaced by one of fear and deceit.

The Destructive Force of Power

Power, when abused, becomes a weapon. It destroys trust, crushes spirits, and leaves a trail of devastation in its wake. In the political arena, we see the chilling effects of power gone wrong. Leaders who once promised hope and change morph into tyrants, their regimes marked by corruption, oppression, and brutality.

Take the infamous case of a dictator who rose to power with promises of prosperity. Once in control, he unleashed a reign of terror. Political opponents were imprisoned or executed. Free speech was stifled, and the media became a mouthpiece for propaganda. The country descended into chaos, with thousands suffering under the weight of his tyranny. His name, once synonymous with hope, became a symbol of fear and oppression.

Power's Capacity to Kill

Power can kill, both literally and metaphorically. In extreme cases, it manifests in acts of violence and genocide. The Rwandan Genocide stands as a stark reminder of power's lethal potential. Political leaders, driven by ethnic hatred and the desire to maintain control, orchestrated a mass slaughter that claimed the lives of over 800,000 people. The chilling efficiency of the genocide, carried out with the support of those in power, remains one of the darkest chapters in human history.

But power can also kill dreams, ambitions and spirits. In corporate environments, abusive leaders can destroy careers, drive talented individuals to burnout, and create toxic workplaces where creativity and innovation are stifled. Employees under such leaders live in constant fear, their potential suffocated by an oppressive atmosphere.

The Humiliation and Embarrassment of Power

Abuse of power not only destroys but also humiliates and embarrasses. Public scandals involving powerful figures lay bare the depths of their moral corruption, stripping them of their dignity and exposing their flaws for all to see. The fall from grace is swift and merciless.

Consider the case of a high-profile media mogul, once revered as a kingmaker in the entertainment industry. His abuse of power, manifested in sexual harassment and coercion, eventually came to light. The ensuing scandal destroyed his career, shattered his legacy, and brought immense embarrassment not just to him, but to the entire industry. The victims, long silenced by his power, finally had a voice, but the damage was already done. His name became synonymous with disgrace, a cautionary tale of how power, when abused, leads to ruin.

The Silent Sufferers

The victims of power abuse often suffer in silence. Their stories are rarely told, their pain hidden behind forced smiles and feigned strength. In workplaces, employees endure harassment, discrimination, and exploitation, afraid to speak out for fear of retaliation. In families, power dynamics can lead to emotional and physical abuse, leaving scars that last a lifetime.

Imagine a young employee, full of potential and eager to learn, becoming the target of a superior's abusive behaviour. The daily harassment, the constant belittling, and the manipulation erode her confidence and self-worth. She becomes a shadow of her former self, her dreams of a thriving career crushed under the weight of her superior's tyranny. Her story, like many others, remains untold, a silent testament to the dark side of power.

The Haunting Legacy of Power Abuse

The legacy of power abuse is long and haunting. It leaves behind broken institutions, devastated communities, and individuals scarred by trauma. The impact of power abuse lingers, often for generations, as trust is hard to rebuild, and the wounds take time to heal.

In the aftermath of such abuse, the road to recovery is fraught with challenges. Institutions must undergo profound changes to restore trust and integrity. Victims need support to heal and rebuild their lives. The process is slow and painful, a stark contrast to the rapid destruction wrought by power abuse.

A Final Warning

Power, when abused, is a dark and destructive force. It has the capacity to destroy lives, careers, and entire societies. The examples in this chapter serve as a chilling reminder of what happens when power is unchecked and wielded without responsibility. For those who hold power, let this be a warning: the path of abuse leads only to ruin and disgrace.

As we reflect on the dark path of power abuse, let us commit to a different kind of leadership – one that is grounded in integrity, empathy, and a deep sense of responsibility. Only then can we harness the true potential of power to uplift, inspire, and create lasting, positive change.

A Transformative Encounter

Early in my career, I worked under a manager who exemplified the abuse of power. His leadership was marked by favouritism, manipulation, and a complete disregard for ethical standards. Witnessing the fear and demoralisation he inflicted on his team was a turning point for me. It solidified my commitment to leading with integrity and ensuring that my use of power would always be in service of others, not at their expense.

The Path to Redemption

For those who have abused power, redemption is possible, but it requires a genuine commitment to change. It involves acknowledging the harm caused, making amends, and striving to rebuild trust. The path to redemption is long and arduous, but it is a crucial step towards healing and restoring integrity.

A Poetic Reflection on Power Abuse

In the shadows where power lies,
A darker path, where virtue dies.
Ambition's fire, when uncontrolled,
Leaves hearts and dreams in ashes cold.

A leader's fall from grace so steep,
In silence, victims' sorrows seep.
Yet from the ruins, hope can rise,
Through humble hearts and tear-filled eyes.

> *For power's touch can heal or scar,*
> *Its true intent, our guiding star.*
> *To lead with heart, to guard the flame,*
> *Ensures that power honours name.*

As we conclude this chapter, let us remember that power is a potent force that must be wielded with care. The stories of abuse serve as stark reminders of the responsibility that comes with power. By committing to ethical leadership and striving to use our influence for good, we can avoid the dark path of power abuse and create a legacy of trust, respect, and positive change.

Chapter Fifteen

Transforming Through True Mentorship

In the intricate journey of personal and professional growth, mentors play an indispensable role. They are the guiding lights who help navigate the complexities of life, offering wisdom, support, and a perspective that expands our horizons. This chapter delves into the transformative power of true mentorship, the profound impact it has had on my life, and examples from around the world that highlight its importance.

The Essence of Mentorship

Mentorship is more than just guidance; it is a relationship built on trust, respect, and a shared vision for growth. A true mentor sees potential where others see challenges and offers encouragement when the path seems most daunting. They provide not only knowledge and experience but also the emotional support that fuels perseverance and resilience. Mentorship is a two-way street: while mentors impart their wisdom, mentees bring fresh perspectives and questions that can also inspire and challenge mentors.

The Importance of Your Circle

Your circle of mentors, colleagues, and friends forms the backbone of your support system. This circle is crucial for expanding your horizons, challenging your perspectives, and pushing you to achieve more than you ever thought possible. The diversity of experiences and insights within your circle fosters innovation and growth, enabling you to see beyond your immediate surroundings and aim higher.

Having a diverse circle means you are exposed to different industries, viewpoints, and life experiences, which can all contribute to a more well-rounded understanding of your own field and personal growth. This network can provide advice and support tailored to your unique needs, helping you navigate both professional and personal challenges.

Traits of a Great Mentor

Great mentors possess certain traits that make them effective guides and catalysts for growth:

1. **Empathy**: They understand your struggles and provide support without judgement.
2. **Experience**: They have a wealth of knowledge and experience to share.
3. **Patience**: They give you the time and space to grow at your own pace.
4. **Honesty**: They provide candid feedback, even when it's hard to hear.
5. **Encouragement**: They inspire confidence and push you to reach your potential.

6. **Accessibility**: They make themselves available and approachable.

Thomas: My Life Coach

Thomas, my life coach, has been a pillar of strength during my most challenging times. When I was on the verge of giving up, Thomas's unwavering belief in me rekindled my spirit. His guidance transcended professional advice; it was deeply personal. Thomas taught me the importance of resilience and the power of a positive mindset. He helped me see that setbacks were not failures, but opportunities to learn and grow. His mentorship was not about solving my problems for me, but about equipping me with the tools and mindset to solve them myself.

Suresh: The Value of Appreciation

Suresh, my first boss, introduced me to the real value of appreciation. Under his mentorship, I learned that recognition and appreciation are powerful motivators. Suresh's leadership style was a blend of encouragement and constructive feedback. He showed me that acknowledging the efforts and achievements of others fosters a positive and productive work environment. This lesson has been instrumental in shaping my approach to leadership, teaching me that a simple 'thank you' can boost morale, inspire loyalty, and hard work.

Colleagues at Tesco, Deloitte, and Other Companies

My journey through various companies like Tesco and Deloitte has been enriched by the mentorship and camaraderie of my colleagues. Each interaction, each shared project brought new insights and learning. These experiences underscored the importance of collaboration and the value of diverse perspectives. My colleagues were not just co-workers; they were mentors in their own right, each contributing to my growth and development. From them, I learned the importance of teamwork and the value of collective wisdom.

My Current Team at Abans

At Abans, my current team continues to inspire and challenge me. Their dedication and innovative thinking push me to strive for excellence. Our collective efforts have not only driven the company forward but also fostered a culture of mutual respect and continuous learning. The mentorship within this team is reciprocal, with each member contributing to and benefiting from our shared knowledge and experience. The synergy we have cultivated proves that mentorship can be horizontal, as well as vertical.

Abhishek: A Boss and a Friend

Abhishek, my boss and dear friend, embodies the essence of true mentorship. His approach to leadership is a blend of professionalism and genuine care. Abhishek has been a constant source of wisdom and support, guiding me through complex decisions and challenging situations. His mentorship has been pivotal in my career, teaching me the importance of balancing ambition with empathy. Abhishek's mentorship style showed me that true leaders are those who lift others up, while striving for their own success.

My Family: The Grounding Force

My family has been my anchor, keeping me grounded and providing unwavering support. Their belief in my abilities has been a source of strength and motivation. They have been my sounding board, offering honest feedback and unconditional love. The values instilled by my family have shaped my character and guided my decisions, both personally and professionally. They remind me that no matter how high I climb, staying true to my roots and values is paramount.

Friends: A Source of Inspiration and Support

Friends like Viraj, Pooja, Nakul, Jheel, Paras, Parth, Unnati, and Vishal have been an integral part of my journey. Their friendship has provided a sense of belonging and support, crucial for my well-being and growth. They have celebrated my successes and stood by me during tough times, their presence a constant reminder of the importance of a strong support network. They have taught me the value of trust and loyalty in relationships, which translates into my professional life as well.

The Universe and My Faith

Beyond individuals, my faith and the universe have played a significant role in my transformation. Believing in a higher power and the interconnectedness of life has given me a sense of purpose and direction. This belief has been a source of comfort and strength, especially during challenging times, reinforcing my resilience and determination. My faith has been my guide, helping me navigate the ups and downs of life with grace and confidence.

The Transformative Power of Mentorship

Reflecting on my journey, it is clear that mentors have been the catalysts for my growth. Their guidance has helped me navigate the complexities of life and career, turning challenges into opportunities. The lessons learned from my mentors have shaped my leadership style, my approach to challenges, and my outlook on life. Mentorship has taught me to view obstacles as opportunities for growth and to always strive for excellence, with integrity.

Global Examples of Mentorship

Mentorship has the power to change lives on a global scale. Consider the story of Oprah Winfrey and her mentor, Maya Angelou. Oprah has often spoken about the profound impact Angelou had on her life, providing wisdom and guidance that helped her navigate the challenges of fame and success. Angelou's mentorship helped Oprah to harness her power responsibly and use it to make a positive impact on the world.

Another powerful example is Steve Jobs and his mentor, Robert Friedland. Jobs met Friedland at Reed College, and Friedland's charismatic and unconventional approach to life left a lasting impression on Jobs. This mentorship helped shape Jobs' innovative thinking and leadership style, contributing to his success at Apple.

Former US President Barack Obama has frequently mentioned the influence of his mentors, including his grandmother, Madelyn Dunham, who raised him and instilled in him the values of hard work and integrity. Obama's journey from community organiser to President was shaped by the mentorship he received along the way, guiding him through the complexities of leadership and public service.

Expanding Horizons Through Mentorship

Mentorship is a dynamic process that continually expands your horizons. By embracing the insights and experiences of others, you gain a broader perspective and a deeper understanding of the world. This expanded horizon is crucial for personal and professional growth, enabling you to navigate the complexities of life with confidence and wisdom.

The Impact of Mentorship on Personal Transformation

Mentorship can profoundly change an individual. It can take a person from a place of uncertainty and fear to one of confidence and clarity. A mentor's belief in your potential can ignite a spark that transforms self-doubt into self-belief. This transformation isn't just about achieving professional success; it's about becoming the best version of yourself.

Consider the story of Malala Yousafzai and her father, Ziauddin Yousafzai. As her mentor, Ziauddin's unwavering support and belief in Malala's right to education fuelled her courage and determination. Despite facing grave dangers, Malala's journey from a small town in Pakistan to becoming a global advocate for girls' education illustrates the transformative power of mentorship. Ziauddin's belief in Malala's potential helped her transcend fear and adversity, empowering her to become a symbol of strength and resilience worldwide.

The Ripple Effect of Mentorship

Mentorship creates a ripple effect where the lessons learned and the values imparted are passed on to others. When you mentor someone, you not only impact their life but also the lives of those they influence. This cascading effect multiplies the positive impact of mentorship, fostering a culture of continuous growth and development.

Consider the story of Sheryl Sandberg, COO of Facebook, and her mentor, Larry Summers. Summers mentored Sandberg during her time at Harvard and later in her career at the World Bank.

Sandberg's mentorship has not only helped her rise to one of the highest positions in tech but also inspired her to mentor countless others, promoting the importance of gender equality and leadership through her book "Lean In" and her public speaking.

Embracing the Mentor

Sometimes, finding the right mentor requires taking the initiative. You must seek out those who inspire you, ask for their guidance, and be open to learning from them. Embracing mentorship means being proactive, recognising that growth often requires stepping out of your comfort zone.

Consider the story of Mark Zuckerberg and his mentor, Bill Gates. Zuckerberg sought out Gates for advice as he navigated the early years of Facebook. This relationship was initiated by Zuckerberg's desire to learn from someone who had successfully scaled a tech company. By embracing Gates as a mentor, Zuckerberg was able to gain invaluable insights that helped shape Facebook's trajectory.

Stories of Ambition: Pratham's Journey of Triumph

In the annals of my career, there are many stories of ambition and success that stand out, but none quite as profoundly as that of Pratham, my first student and mentee. His journey from a young, determined learner to the founder of Zell Education, an innovative edtech company specialising in professional qualifications, is a shining example of the power of resolve and mental strength.

Pratham's story began in a modest classroom where he exhibited a keen understanding and a relentless curiosity for academics. From the very beginning, he showed an extraordinary ability to grasp complex concepts and a determination that set him apart from his peers. I saw in him a spark that, with the right guidance and support, could ignite a transformative journey.

Our mentor-mentee relationship flourished through countless discussions, late-night study sessions, and moments of doubt and triumph. Pratham's unwavering dedication to his studies and his ambition to make a significant impact in the world of education were clear. He was not just a student; he was a visionary in the making.

Years later, Pratham founded Zell Education, an edtech company that has since revolutionised professional qualifications. Zell's innovative approach and commitment to quality education have made it a beacon for aspiring professionals. Pratham and Zell hold a special place in my heart, not only because of their success, but also because they embody the powerful feeling of being a mentor.

I often visit Zell, making appearances to support and celebrate its growth. The success of Pratham and Zell brings me immense pride and strengthens the bond we share as mentor and mentee. It's moments like these that remind me of the true power of mentorship.

A Conversation with Pratham

One afternoon, as I sat in Zell's vibrant office, Pratham joined me for a chat. Our conversation turned to the journey we had shared and the lessons learned along the way.

Nirbhay:, "Pratham, I still remember our first meeting. You had that spark in your eyes and an insatiable curiosity. Did you ever imagine you'd come this far?"

Pratham: (Smiling) "Honestly, Nirbhay, I always had big dreams, but it was the belief that made all the difference. You taught me the technical skills and helped me develop a vision to see the bigger picture."

Nirbhay: "And look at you now, leading Zell Education. What has been the most rewarding part of this journey for you?"

Pratham: "Seeing the impact we're making on students' lives. Every success story from Zell feels personal. It's like watching a part of my dream come true in their achievements. And having you here, still guiding and supporting us, makes it even more special."

Nirbhay: "That's the beauty of mentorship, Pratham. It's a lifelong relationship. I see in Zell the same passion and commitment to education that you showed as a student. What advice would you give to young leaders who are just starting out?"

Pratham: "I'd say, always stay curious and never be afraid to ask questions. Seek out mentors who believe in you and are willing to guide you. And, most importantly, be resilient. There will be challenges, but it's how you overcome them that defines your success."

Nirbhay: "Wise words. Mentorship is a two-way street. I've learned as much from you as you have from me. Watching you grow has been one of the most rewarding experiences of my career."

Pratham: "Thank you, Nirbhay. Your guidance has been invaluable. I hope to inspire and mentor others just as you have inspired me."

Nirbhay: "And you will, Pratham. You're already doing it through Zell. Remember, the true measure of success is the number of lives you've touched and transformed. You're on the right path."

Our conversation that day was a reflection of the journey we had shared and the promise of many more achievements to come.

Pratham's story is a beacon for young leaders, demonstrating that with determination, the right guidance, and an unwavering belief in oneself, anything is possible. His journey is a symbol of the transformative power of mentorship and the enduring impact it can have on both mentor and mentee.

Conclusion

The transformative power of true mentorship cannot be overstated. It is through the guidance, support, and wisdom of mentors that we grow, evolve, and reach our fullest potential. As you reflect on your journey, recognise the mentors who have shaped your path and seek out those who can guide you further. In the end, it is the collective wisdom and support of your circle that will propel you towards success and fulfilment.

Mentorship is not just a tool for professional advancement; it is a beacon of personal growth and transformation. It challenges us to push our boundaries, to strive for excellence, and to become mentors ourselves, continuing the cycle of growth and development. Embrace the mentors in your life, seek out new ones, and become a mentor to others. In this way, we can all contribute to a world where true mentorship transforms lives and fosters a culture of continuous improvement and mutual support.

The journey of mentorship is ongoing. As you grow, your needs will change, and so will your mentors. Be open to evolving, to learning from different people at different stages of your life. The right mentor can make all the difference, helping you navigate the twists and turns of life with wisdom and grace. Let mentorship be the compass that guides you towards a future filled with growth, success, and fulfilment.

Letters from My Mentors

Thomas: A Beacon of Resilience and Support

Nirbhay - My Friend

I have known Nirbhay for the last ten years, and during this time, he has proven to be nothing short of a "Financial Wizard" at such a young age. When I first met him a decade ago, he was already the second-in-command at one of the largest companies. Nirbhay is truly a master at what he does. Any company can rest assured that it is in safe hands with him, as he has an innate ability to churn out profits from seemingly nowhere.

What sets Nirbhay apart from other leaders is his calm and helping aura. He genuinely sees and feels the pain of others, which is a rare trait in the corporate world. Unlike most leaders I have encountered, Nirbhay has a remarkable ability to think from his heart while still performing magic with numbers and profits. He is a great friend to have and an exceptional leader.

A Personal Reflection

Everyone experiences ups and downs in life, and Nirbhay, one of the greatest leaders I have seen, is no exception. However, the difference with Nirbhay is his deeply embedded "Never Give Up" attitude. During his low moments, he reached out to me, and I witnessed his incredible resilience as he bounced back with immense power, energy, confidence, and determination. This rebound is worth studying as a case study in itself. How a man can rise with such tremendous

"Light & Love" and then extend that light and love to others in need is something everyone should learn from Nirbhay.

Suresh: The Mentor Who Saw My Potential

Nirbhay - The Visionary

I remember the first time I met Nirbhay as a new recruit. There was a spark in his eyes, a burning eagerness to learn and take on responsibilities. Even in his early days, he displayed an extraordinary ability to solve problems. He had a vision, and I was certain that Nirbhay was destined for greater things.

As his mentor, I have had the privilege of watching him grow and evolve. Every time he calls to discuss his professional and personal life, I am never surprised by his achievements. Nirbhay's journey has been a testament to his dedication and vision. I am extremely humbled to be mentioned in this remarkable book about his journey of leadership. It is an honor to be a part of his story and witness his transformation through true mentorship.

These letters reflect the profound impact my mentors have had on my life, shaping me into the leader I am today. Their guidance, support, and unwavering belief in my potential have been invaluable. Each mentor has left an indelible mark on my journey, and their lessons continue to inspire and motivate me as I strive to lead with empathy, resilience, and vision.

Chapter Sixteen

Leadership in Crisis - Navigating Storms

Leadership is often tested in the crucible of crisis. It is during these tumultuous times that true leaders emerge, navigating through the storms with resilience and clarity. I've noticed that individuals who have faced significant challenges in their early lives often excel during crises, while those who have had more secure upbringings may struggle. This chapter explores how one's childhood and early experiences shape their ability to lead in times of crisis, drawing on examples from various environments, including mythology, corporate worlds, political arenas, and historical struggles. This chapter aims to prepare leaders for crises by explaining how crises can occur, identifying wrong behaviours during such periods, and offering strategies for effective leadership.

The Impact of Childhood on Crisis Management

Childhood experiences play a pivotal role in shaping one's ability to handle crises. Those who have faced adversity early in life develop a unique resilience and adaptability. They learn to thrive under pressure, finding comfort in chaos because they have been there before. On the other hand, individuals with more secure childhoods may find crises overwhelming, as they are unaccustomed to such instability.

Understanding Crises: How They Occur

Crises can emerge from various sources, often when least expected. Understanding the potential origins of a crisis can help leaders prepare and respond more effectively:

1. **Economic Downturns**: Financial instability, market crashes, or economic recessions can create significant turmoil within organisations.
2. **Regulatory Changes**: Sudden changes in laws or regulations can disrupt operations and force organisations to rapidly adapt.
3. **Internal Fraud**: Misconduct or unethical behaviour within an organisation can lead to scandals and loss of trust.
4. **Natural Disasters**: Events such as earthquakes, floods, or pandemics can cause widespread disruption and necessitate immediate action.
5. **Technological Failures**: Cyberattacks, data breaches, or system failures can cripple operations and compromise security.

Wrong Behaviours During a Crisis

In times of crisis, certain behaviours can exacerbate the situation and hinder effective resolution. Recognising and avoiding these pitfalls is crucial for leaders:

1. **Panic and Overreaction**: Reacting impulsively or with panic can create chaos and undermine confidence.

2. **Denial and Inaction**: Ignoring the crisis or delaying action can allow the situation to worsen.
3. **Blame Shifting**: Pointing fingers and avoiding responsibility erodes trust and morale.
4. **Poor Communication**: Lack of transparency and unclear messaging can lead to confusion and distrust.
5. **Isolation**: Trying to handle the crisis alone without seeking input or support can result in poor decision-making and burnout.

Effective Crisis Management: How to React When Everyone Is Jumping Ship

When a crisis hits, and everyone seems to be jumping ship, effective leadership is critical. Here are strategies to navigate such turbulent times:

1. **Stay Calm and Focused**: Maintain composure and focus on the immediate priorities. Your calm demeanour will help reassure and stabilise your team.
2. **Communicate Transparently**: Provide clear, honest, and timely updates about the situation. Transparency builds trust and keeps everyone informed.
3. **Show Empathy and Support**: Acknowledge the concerns and fears of your team. Show empathy and provide support to those affected.
4. **Take Decisive Action**: Make informed decisions swiftly. Demonstrating confidence and decisiveness helps to restore confidence.
5. **Engage and Involve Your Team**: Involve your team in problem-solving. Encourage collaboration and leverage their expertise and perspectives.

6. **Focus on Solutions**: Shift the focus from the problem to potential solutions. Encourage a proactive and optimistic mindset.

Attracting People Towards You When Trust Is Low

Building and maintaining trust during a crisis is challenging but essential. Here are strategies to attract and retain trust:

1. **Lead by Example**: Demonstrate integrity, accountability, and resilience. Your actions will set the tone for your team.
2. **Be Transparent**: Share information openly and honestly. Transparency fosters trust and credibility.
3. **Listen Actively**: Show that you value input from others by actively listening and considering their perspectives.
4. **Provide Consistent Support**: Be present and supportive consistently. Show that you are committed to the well-being of your team.
5. **Celebrate Small Wins**: Recognise and celebrate progress, no matter how small. Celebrations boost morale and reinforce a sense of achievement.

Examples of Leadership in Crisis

Mythological Crisis: Odysseus and the Trojan War

In Greek mythology, Odysseus faced numerous crises during and after the Trojan War. Known for his cunning and resourcefulness, he led his men through perilous situations, including the encounter with the Cyclops and navigating past the Sirens. Odysseus's ability to remain calm, think strategically, and inspire his men showcases timeless leadership qualities essential during crises.

Corporate Crisis: Johnson & Johnson and the Tylenol Poisonings

In 1982, Johnson & Johnson faced a severe crisis when seven people died after taking cyanide-laced Tylenol capsules. The company's CEO, James Burke, took immediate and decisive action. He ordered a nationwide recall of Tylenol products, communicated transparently with the public, and introduced tamper-resistant packaging. Burke's leadership during this crisis not only saved the company but also set a new standard for crisis management in the industry.

Political Crisis: Winston Churchill and World War II

During World War II, Winston Churchill faced the monumental task of leading Britain through one of its darkest periods. His powerful speeches, unwavering resolve, and strategic alliances inspired the British people and maintained morale. Churchill's leadership demonstrated the importance of clear communication, resilience, and strategic foresight in overcoming a national crisis.

"If you are going through hell, keep going."

–Winston Churchill.

Historical Crisis: Franklin D. Roosevelt and the Great Depression

Franklin D. Roosevelt assumed the presidency during the Great Depression, a time of unprecedented economic turmoil. Through his New Deal programmes, he provided immediate relief, enacted financial reforms, and created jobs. Roosevelt's ability to communicate hope and implement comprehensive strategies helped steer the nation towards recovery.

"The only thing we have to fear is fear itself,"

—Franklin D. Roosevelt.

The **Inspiring Turnaround** of Tata Motors

In the late 2000s, Tata Motors, one of India's largest and most respected automobile manufacturers, faced a severe economic and market crisis. The company, known for its innovative and reliable vehicles, was hit hard by a global economic downturn, increasing competition, and internal challenges. Sales plummeted, and the company's financial health deteriorated rapidly. Tata Motors was on the brink of significant financial distress, and the future looked uncertain.

The Leader: Cyrus Mistry

Cyrus Mistry, who took over as Chairman of Tata Motors in 2012, stepped up during this critical time. With a background in engineering and extensive experience within the Tata Group, Mistry brought a strategic mindset and a fresh perspective. He understood the importance of resilience, innovation, and strategic thinking. Mistry saw the crisis not as a death knell, but as an opportunity for transformation.

The Challenge

Tata Motors' crisis was multifaceted. The company was burdened with high operational costs, an ageing product lineup, and a declining market share. The financial situation was precarious, with significant losses and dwindling cash reserves. Employee morale was low, and trust in the leadership was eroding. The automotive giant needed a radical turnaround to survive.

Strategy and Action

1. **Transparent Communication:** Mistry understood that transparency was key to restoring trust and rallying the workforce. He held regular town hall meetings, transparently sharing the severity of the crisis and the steps they needed to take. Mistry emphasised that every employee's input was valuable, fostering a sense of collective responsibility. He communicated openly about the financial challenges, the need for change, and the potential consequences if Tata Motors did not adapt.

2. **Decisive Actions:** Mistry quickly implemented a comprehensive restructuring plan. He streamlined operations, focusing on the core Tata brand and divesting non-core assets. Cost-cutting measures were put in place, including closing underperforming plants and renegotiating supplier contracts. Despite the financial constraints, Mistry prioritised retaining key talent and minimising layoffs.

3. **Engaging the Team:** Mistry introduced a unified strategy that aimed to align all employees with a common vision and set of goals. He formed cross-functional teams to foster collaboration and innovation. These teams were tasked with identifying areas for improvement and developing new ideas to drive efficiency and growth. This inclusive approach not only generated creative solutions but also empowered employees, making them feel integral to the company's revival.

4. **Focus on Innovation:** Investing in product development was a risky but necessary move. Mistry redirected resources to develop a new lineup of fuel-efficient and electric vehicles,

including the Tata Nano and the Tata Nexon EV. He fostered a culture of innovation, encouraging and rewarding employees for creative ideas that improved product design and performance. This shift in focus not only helped Tata Motors meet changing consumer demands, but also positioned the company as a leader in sustainability.

5. **Building Trust:** Throughout the crisis, Mistry maintained open lines of communication. He regularly updated the company on progress, challenges, and successes. Celebrating small wins, such as achieving a new milestone in vehicle development, or securing a critical partnership, helped rebuild trust and boost morale. Mistry's consistent and transparent communication reassured employees that they were all in this together.

6. **External Partnerships:** Understanding the importance of external support, Mistry strengthened relationships with suppliers, dealers, and government bodies. He formed strategic partnerships that provided Tata Motors with the guidance and resources needed to navigate the regulatory landscape. These collaborations not only helped Tata Motors comply with environmental regulations, but also enhanced its reputation as a forward-thinking company dedicated to sustainability.

The Outcome

Under Cyrus Mistry's leadership, Tata Motors not only survived the crisis but emerged stronger. The company's new lineup of fuel-efficient and electric vehicles received critical acclaim and drove a resurgence in sales and profitability. The innovative solutions developed during the crisis led to long-term efficiencies, significantly reducing operational costs.

Employee morale soared as the company navigated its way out of the crisis. Trust within the organisation was restored, and Tata Motors was recognised as a leader in both the automotive industry and corporate sustainability. Mistry's leadership during this turbulent period transformed Tata Motors, turning a potential downfall into a story of resilience, innovation, and collective triumph.

Developing a Formula for Crisis Management

Based on these examples and my personal experiences, here is a practical formula for effective crisis management:

1. **Assess the Situation**:
   - Gather accurate information.
   - Understand the scope and impact of the crisis.
2. **Stay Calm and Focused**:
   - Maintain composure.
   - Prioritise immediate actions.
3. **Communicate Transparently**:
   - Provide clear and honest updates.
   - Foster open communication channels.
4. **Show Empathy and Support**:
   - Acknowledge concerns.
   - Offer support and reassurance.
5. **Take Decisive Action**:
   - Make informed decisions quickly.
   - Demonstrate confidence.
6. **Engage and Involve the Team**:
   - Collaborate and seek input.

- Leverage team expertise.

7. **Focus on Solutions**:
    - Shift from problem identification to solution generation.
    - Encourage proactive and optimistic thinking.

8. **Build and Maintain Trust**:
    - Lead by example.
    - Be transparent and accessible.

9. **Celebrate Progress**:
    - Recognise and celebrate small wins.
    - Maintain morale and motivation.

10. **Plan for Future Resilience**:
    - Develop contingency plans.
    - Foster a culture of adaptability and continuous learning.

Conclusion

Navigating storms is an essential part of leadership. The ability to lead effectively during crises often stems from early life experiences that foster resilience and adaptability. Whether in the workplace, political arena, or home, true leaders shine brightest when faced with adversity. By understanding how crises occur, recognising wrong behaviours, and adopting effective crisis management strategies, leaders can prepare themselves to navigate any storm with confidence and grace.

Leadership in a crisis is not just about survival; it's about emerging stronger and more resilient. It is in these moments of turmoil that the true essence of leadership is revealed, inspiring others and paving the way for a brighter future. By embracing the lessons of crisis management and fostering a culture of resilience, leaders can turn challenges into opportunities and guide their teams to success.

As we reflect on the inspiring stories of leaders like Emily Hartman of Zenith Industries, Winston Churchill, and Franklin D. Roosevelt, it becomes clear that the qualities of transparency, empathy, decisive action, and innovative thinking are crucial for leading through crises. These leaders demonstrated that it is possible to overcome even the most daunting challenges by staying focused, communicating clearly, and engaging their teams.

In the words of Nelson Mandela, "The greatest glory in living lies not in never falling, but in rising every time we fall." This quote encapsulates the spirit of resilient leadership. As leaders, we must embrace crises as opportunities to rise, learn, and grow. By preparing ourselves and our teams to handle crises with strength and determination, we can build organisations and communities that are not only resilient, but also thrive in the face of adversity.

In conclusion, let the lessons of history, mythology, and modern-day crises serve as a guide. Adopt the formula for crisis management, stay calm and focused, communicate transparently, show empathy, take decisive action, involve your team, focus on solutions, build and maintain trust, celebrate progress, and plan for future resilience. These principles will not only help you navigate through storms but also emerge as a stronger, more capable leader, ready to face any challenge that comes your way.

Remember, true leadership is tested in times of crisis. Your ability to steer through the storm with resilience, empathy, and strategic foresight will define your legacy and inspire those who follow you. Embrace the challenge, lead with courage, and turn crises into opportunities for growth and transformation.

Chapter Seventeen

Leadership Integrity: The Bedrock of Trust

In the landscape of leadership, integrity stands as the bedrock upon which trust is built. While various traits contribute to effective leadership, integrity is the one that cements a leader's credibility, fosters loyalty, and guides ethical decision-making. This chapter delves into the critical role of integrity in leadership, exploring how it influences actions, strengthens organizations, and sustains long-term success.

The Role of Integrity in Leadership

Integrity involves more than just honesty; it encompasses a consistent adherence to moral and ethical principles, even when faced with difficult choices. Leaders who demonstrate integrity earn the respect and trust of their teams, creating a culture where ethical behavior is not just expected but embodied at every level.

Case Study: Ursula Burns, Former CEO of Xerox: Ursula Burns exemplified leadership integrity during her tenure at Xerox. Tasked with transforming the company in a challenging business environment, Burns faced numerous tough decisions. Her commitment to transparency and ethical conduct, even when it required difficult conversations and decisions, helped steer Xerox through its transition while maintaining the trust and respect of her employees and stakeholders. Burns' leadership integrity was instrumental in ensuring that the company's transformation was not just effective, but also ethical.

Integrity in Decision-Making: The Foundation of Ethical Leadership

Decisions made with integrity are guided by a strong moral compass, ensuring that the actions taken are in the best interest of the organization and its stakeholders. Leaders who prioritize integrity in their decision-making processes build a foundation of trust that supports long-term success.

Personal Experience:

In my own leadership journey, I have faced moments where the pressure to compromise on ethical standards was immense. One such instance involved a lucrative business opportunity that, if pursued, would have required bending our organization's ethical guidelines. Choosing integrity over short-term gains was not easy, but it reinforced a culture of trust within the organization. This decision, though challenging at the time, laid the groundwork for sustainable growth and a reputation built on ethical leadership.

Integrity in Crisis Management: Upholding Ethical Standards Under Pressure

Crisis situations often test the integrity of leaders. In such moments, the true character of a leader is revealed through their ability to uphold ethical standards, even when the pressure to do otherwise is overwhelming.

Case Study: Mary Barra, CEO of General Motors: Mary Barra's leadership during the GM ignition switch crisis is a prime example of integrity under pressure. Faced with a recall that implicated the company in several deaths, Barra chose to act with transparency and responsibility. She publicly acknowledged the issue, took decisive action to address it, and implemented long-term changes to prevent future occurrences. Barra's integrity in handling the crisis restored trust in GM's commitment to safety and ethics, demonstrating that integrity is crucial in crisis management.

The Interplay of Integrity and Empathy: A Balanced Approach

While this chapter emphasizes integrity, it's important to recognize that integrity is often complemented by empathy. Leaders who integrate empathy with integrity are better equipped to make ethical decisions that also consider the human impact. This balance helps create a leadership style that is both principled and compassionate.

Case Study: Sundar Pichai, CEO of Alphabet Inc.:

Sundar Pichai's leadership during the 2018 Google walkout illustrates how integrity and empathy can work together to guide a company through challenging situations. By acknowledging employees' concerns and addressing them with a commitment to ethical practices, Pichai reinforced both the moral and human dimensions of leadership, ultimately strengthening Google's organizational culture.

Sustaining Integrity in Leadership: Building a Culture of Trust

Leaders who embody integrity not only set an example but also inspire their teams to adhere to the same standards. Building and sustaining a culture of integrity requires consistent effort, clear communication, and a commitment to holding oneself and others accountable.

Case Study: Tim Cook, CEO of Apple:

Tim Cook's leadership at Apple reflects a sustained commitment to integrity. Under his guidance, Apple has navigated complex ethical challenges, from data privacy concerns to supply chain practices, with a focus on maintaining ethical standards. Cook's integrity has been key to Apple's ability to retain customer trust and loyalty, proving that integrity is not just a leadership trait, but a strategic asset.

Building a Roadmap to Fulfilled Leadership

Empathy and integrity should be at the core of every leader's philosophy. Here's a roadmap to integrating these values into your leadership style:

1. **Cultivate Self-Awareness**: Understand your own values, strengths, and weaknesses. Reflect on your actions and decisions regularly to ensure they align with your principles.

2. **Practice Active Listening**: Show genuine interest in your team's concerns and perspectives. Listen more than you speak, and acknowledge their feelings and viewpoints.
3. **Lead by Example**: Demonstrate integrity in all your actions. Be transparent, honest, and consistent in your behaviour.
4. **Foster a Culture of Empathy**: Encourage empathy within your team. Create an environment where people feel safe to express their concerns and where their well-being is prioritised.
5. **Hold Yourself and Others Accountable**: Set high ethical standards and ensure that everyone, including yourself, adheres to them. Address unethical behaviour promptly and fairly.
6. **Communicate with Clarity and Compassion**: Be clear and transparent in your communication. Deliver tough messages with empathy, and always be open to feedback.
7. **Empower Your Team**: Trust your team members and give them the autonomy to make decisions. Support their growth and development.
8. **Celebrate Integrity and Empathy**: Recognise and reward behaviours that reflect empathy and integrity. Make these values a central part of your organisational culture.

Conclusion

Integrity is the cornerstone of effective and enduring leadership. It is the quality that ensures leaders make decisions that are not only effective but also ethical. While empathy complements integrity, it is integrity that builds the foundation of trust, credibility, and respect that every leader needs to succeed. As you continue on your leadership journey, remember that integrity is not just about doing the right thing—it's about consistently embodying the values and principles that define true leadership.

Reflecting on my own journey, I am convinced that empathy and integrity are not just ideals to strive for, but essential qualities that define true leadership. They are the threads that weave together the fabric of a successful and enduring legacy. As leaders, let us commit to embracing empathy and integrity, not only for the success of our organisations, but for the betterment of the people we lead and the communities we serve.

In the words of Maya Angelou, "People will forget what you said, people will forget what you did, but people will never forget how you made them feel." And in the words of C.S. Lewis, "Integrity is doing the right thing, even when no one is watching." These quotes remind us of the lasting impact of leading with empathy and integrity, shaping not just the success of our endeavours, but the very fabric of our shared humanity.

As you continue on your leadership journey, let empathy and integrity be your guiding lights. They will help you navigate challenges, build strong and loyal teams, and create a lasting and positive impact. Embrace these values, and you will find that they not only lead to a fulfilled leadership, but also inspire those around you to strive for the same.

Chapter Eighteen

Building Resilience: Lessons from Failure

Leadership is not always going to be rainbows and sunshine. We all fail, and we might fail more often than we succeed. But it is through these failures that we build resilience and learn the most valuable lessons in leadership. This chapter delves into the importance of failure, drawing on the experiences of some of the most successful leaders in the world, including my personal journey. Embracing failure not only makes us real but also transforms us into better leaders.

The Power of Failure

Failure is often seen as a setback, but in reality, it is a powerful teacher. It forces us to confront our weaknesses, rethink our strategies, and adapt to new challenges. Consider Roger Federer, who said, "I have failed more times than I have succeeded, and I am still here today." Despite numerous losses and injuries, Federer never lost faith. Each defeat was a lesson, pushing him to refine his skills and approach. His resilience turned every setback into a stepping stone towards greatness.

Roger Federer: Learning from Defeat: Federer's journey is a testament to how failure can pave the way for greatness. He experienced countless losses and setbacks, yet he always saw these as opportunities to learn and improve. "I've missed more shots than I've made," Federer once reflected. "But each miss was a lesson, a chance to get better, to understand my game more deeply." His ability to embrace failure, learn from it, and persist is what has made him one of the greatest tennis players of all time.

Learning from the Failures of Great Leaders

The most successful leaders have all faced significant failures. What sets them apart is their ability to learn from these experiences and emerge stronger.

- **Steve Jobs: The Comeback King**: Steve Jobs, co-founder of Apple, experienced a dramatic failure when he was ousted from his own company in 1985. Reflecting on this period, Jobs said, "It was awful tasting medicine, but I guess the patient needed it. Sometimes life hits you in the head with a brick. Don't lose faith." Jobs acknowledged his failures, used the experience to innovate with NeXT and Pixar, and eventually returned to Apple, leading it to unprecedented success. His story teaches us that acknowledging failure is the first step to overcoming it and using it as fuel for future success.

- **Walt Disney: Imagination Reborn**: Walt Disney was once fired from a newspaper job for "lacking imagination" and faced bankruptcy with his first animation company. Disney once remarked, "I think it's important to have a good, hard failure when you're young. I learned a lot out of that." Instead of being deterred, Disney used these early failures to fuel his creative vision, eventually founding one of the most successful entertainment empires in the world. His resilience and ability to learn from setbacks exemplify the transformative power of failure.

- **Oprah Winfrey: Turning Setbacks into Strength**: Oprah Winfrey was demoted from her job as a news anchor because she wasn't fit for television. Reflecting on this failure, Winfrey said, "There is no such thing as failure. Failure is just life trying to move us in another direction." This experience led her to launch her own talk show, which became a groundbreaking success. Winfrey's journey underscores the importance of recognising failures as redirections towards greater opportunities.

My Journey: Embracing Failures

My path has been shaped significantly by my failures. Failing at exams, outcomes, meetings, and work has made me the leader I am today. These experiences have provided invaluable lessons that have helped me grow and improve continuously.

- **Failure at Exams**: During my academic journey, I faced several setbacks. There were exams I didn't pass and subjects I struggled with. Each failure taught me the importance of perseverance and hard work. It pushed me to develop better study habits and time management skills, which have been crucial in my professional life. Acknowledging these failures and understanding what went wrong allowed me to make necessary adjustments and, eventually, succeed.

- **Failure at Outcomes**: In my career, there have been numerous projects that didn't go as planned. These failures taught me the importance of adaptability and resilience. Instead of being discouraged, I used these experiences to reassess my strategies, seek feedback, and make necessary adjustments. Each failed project became a learning experience that helped refine my approach and improve future outcomes.

- **Failure at Meetings**: Not every meeting has been a success. There were times when I couldn't convey my ideas effectively or secure the desired outcome. These experiences taught me the importance of preparation and effective communication. They pushed me to become a better speaker and listener. By acknowledging these shortcomings, I was able to work on my communication skills and approach meetings with greater confidence and clarity.

- **Failure at Work**: Throughout my career, I've encountered professional failures that seemed insurmountable at the time. Each failure, however, provided a learning opportunity. They taught me the importance of empathy, integrity, and continuous improvement. These lessons have not only shaped my leadership style but also made me a better mentor and guide for my team. Recognising and addressing these failures head-on allowed me to grow and lead with greater authenticity and effectiveness.

The Role of Failure in Leadership Development

Failures play a crucial role in leadership development. They provide the following benefits:

1. **Humility and Realism**: Failure keeps leaders humble and grounded. It reminds us that we are not infallible and that there is always room for improvement.

2. **Resilience and Persistence**: Facing failures builds resilience and teaches us to persist in the face of adversity.

3. **Innovation and Creativity**: Failure often forces us to think outside the box and come up with innovative solutions.

4. **Empathy and Understanding**: Leaders who have experienced failure are more empathetic and understanding towards their team's struggles.

5. **Continuous Learning**: Failure promotes a culture of continuous learning and improvement. It encourages leaders to seek feedback, learn from their mistakes, and strive for better outcomes.

Building Resilience Through Failure: A Roadmap

1. **Acknowledge and Accept Failure**: The first step in building resilience is acknowledging and accepting failure. Understand that failure is a natural part of the journey and an opportunity to learn. Recognise the role you played in the failure and be honest about what went wrong.

2. **Analyse and Reflect**: Take the time to analyse what went wrong. Reflect on the factors that contributed to the failure and identify areas for improvement. Ask yourself what you could have done differently and what lessons you can take away from the experience.

3. **Seek Feedback**: Don't be afraid to seek feedback from others. Constructive feedback provides valuable insights and helps you understand different perspectives. Use this feedback to inform your future actions and decisions.

4. **Learn and Adapt**: Use the lessons learned from failure to adapt your strategies and approaches. Be open to change

and willing to try new methods. Flexibility and adaptability are key to overcoming future challenges.

5. **Stay Positive and Persistent**: Maintain a positive attitude and stay persistent. Remember that each failure brings you one step closer to success. Cultivate a growth mindset and view setbacks as opportunities for growth and development.

6. **Support Your Team**: As a leader, support your team in their failures. Encourage a culture where failure is seen as a learning opportunity and provide the necessary support to help them grow. Lead by example and show that it is okay to fail, as long as you learn from it and keep moving forward.

Inspiring Quotes on Failure

Incorporating the wisdom of great leaders into our narrative helps illustrate the power of failure:

- **Michael Jordan**: "I've missed more than 9,000 shots in my career. I've lost almost 300 games. Twenty-six times, I've been trusted to take the game-winning shot and missed. I've failed over and over and over again in my life. And that is why I succeed." Jordan's career exemplifies how embracing failure and learning from it can lead to greatness.

- **J.K. Rowling**: "It is impossible to live without failing at something, unless you live so cautiously that you might as well not have lived at all—in which case, you fail by default." Rowling's journey from a struggling writer to a best-selling author demonstrates that failure can be a catalyst for achieving one's dreams.

- **Thomas Edison**: "I have not failed. I've just found 10,000 ways that won't work." Edison's relentless experimentation and refusal to see setbacks as failures led to some of the greatest inventions of our time.

Conclusion

Building resilience through failure is an essential part of leadership. It is not always going to be rainbows and sunshine, but it is through these storms that we grow stronger and wiser. Embracing failure, learning from it, and using it as a stepping stone to success is what differentiates great leaders from the rest.

Failures are not the end, but the beginning of a journey towards growth and excellence. They make us real, keep us grounded, and continuously push us to become better versions of ourselves. As you continue on your leadership journey, remember that each failure is an opportunity to learn, adapt, and build resilience.

In the words of Winston Churchill, "Success is not final, failure is not fatal: It is the courage to continue that counts." Let this be your guiding principle as you navigate the challenges and failures that come your way. Embrace them, learn from them, and let them propel you towards greater heights.

Cultural Leadership: Embracing Diversity

Leadership transcends titles and positions; it is about inspiring and empowering others, embracing diversity, and championing equality. In the context of India and the world, cultural leadership is about acknowledging and celebrating differences while fostering an environment where everyone has the opportunity to thrive. This chapter delves into the importance of cultural leadership, focusing on gender equality, the broader spectrum of diversity, and the challenges and triumphs of embracing an inclusive approach.

The Essence of Cultural Leadership

Cultural leadership involves understanding, respecting, and valuing the diverse backgrounds and perspectives of those we lead. It requires a commitment to creating inclusive environments where everyone feels valued and respected. In India, a country known for its rich cultural tapestry, embracing diversity is not just beneficial, but essential for true progress.

Embracing Gender Diversity

Despite significant progress, women around the world continue to face barriers to leadership. In India, traditional gender roles and societal expectations often limit women's opportunities. However, women who overcome these barriers can become powerful leaders and advocates for change.

Personal Experience: My Feminist Journey: As a feminist, I have often been questioned by conventional leadership for my beliefs in gender equality. But my conviction in an equal world drives me to challenge these norms and advocate for change. Feminism is not about elevating women above men; it is about ensuring that everyone, regardless of gender, has the same opportunities and respect.

Case Study: Kiran Mazumdar-Shaw: Kiran Mazumdar-Shaw, the founder of Biocon, is a trailblazer in the Indian biotech industry. Despite facing scepticism and gender bias, she built one of India's largest biopharmaceutical companies. Mazumdar-Shaw's success is a testament to the power of perseverance and the importance of challenging societal norms. Her leadership has not only advanced the biotech field but also inspired countless women to pursue their dreams.

Embracing Ethnic and Cultural Diversity

Ethnic and cultural diversity enriches organisations with a variety of perspectives and ideas. However, discrimination based on ethnicity or cultural background remains a significant barrier to true inclusivity.

Case Study: Sundar Pichai: Sundar Pichai, CEO of Alphabet Inc., hails from Chennai, India. His rise to one of the highest positions in the tech industry highlights the importance of embracing ethnic diversity. Pichai's leadership style, characterised by empathy and humility, has been instrumental in Google's success. He often speaks about his immigrant experience and advocates for policies that support diversity and inclusion within the tech industry.

Embracing LGBTQ+ Diversity

The LGBTQ+ community faces unique challenges, including discrimination and a lack of representation in leadership roles. Embracing LGBTQ+ diversity means creating a safe and supportive environment where everyone can be their authentic selves.

Case Study: Tim Cook: Tim Cook, CEO of Apple, publicly came out as gay in 2014, making him one of the few openly gay CEOs of a major company. Cook's decision was a powerful statement about the importance of LGBTQ+ representation in leadership. He has used his platform to advocate for LGBTQ+ rights and promote inclusivity within Apple and beyond.

Embracing Neurodiversity

Neurodiversity refers to the inclusion of individuals with neurological differences, such as autism, ADHD, and dyslexia. Embracing neurodiversity means recognising and valuing the unique strengths and perspectives these individuals bring.

Case Study: SAP's Autism at Work Programme: SAP, a global software company, launched the Autism at Work programme to hire individuals on the autism spectrum. The programme recognises the unique skills and perspectives that neurodiverse individuals can bring to the workplace. SAP's commitment to neurodiversity has led to increased innovation and problem-solving capabilities within the company.

The Challenges of Embracing Diversity

While embracing diversity is essential, it is not without challenges. Societal norms, biases and discrimination often create barriers to true inclusivity.

- **Injustice and Inequality in Indian Homes**: In India, the home is often the first place where issues of injustice and inequality manifest. These deeply rooted cultural and societal norms can crush dreams and limit opportunities.

- **The Treatment of Women**: Women in India often face significant challenges within their own homes. Traditional gender roles dictate that women prioritise domestic responsibilities over education and career aspirations. This expectation not only limits their personal growth but also perpetuates a cycle of dependence and inequality.

- **Case Study: Domestic Injustice**: Consider the story of Meera, a young woman from a small village in India. Despite being an excellent student, Meera was forced to abandon her education to take care of her younger siblings and manage household chores. Her dreams of becoming a teacher were crushed by the weight of traditional expectations. Meera's story is not unique; countless women across India face similar struggles, their potential stifled by societal norms.

- **Casteism: A Barrier to Equality**: Casteism remains a pervasive issue in India, affecting millions of lives. The caste system, though officially abolished, still influences social interactions, access to resources, and opportunities. Lower-caste individuals often face discrimination, limiting their educational and professional prospects.

- **Case Study: Educational Inequality**: Take the case of Ravi, a bright student from a Dalit (lower-caste) family. Despite his academic prowess, Ravi faced constant discrimination and bullying at school. His teachers overlooked his potential, and his classmates ostracised him. These barriers significantly hindered Ravi's educational journey, illustrating how casteism can crush dreams and perpetuate inequality.

Global Perspectives: Learning from International Leaders

Globally, there are numerous examples of leaders who have embraced diversity and championed equality.

Jacinda Ardern: Leading with Compassion: Jacinda Ardern, the former Prime Minister of New Zealand, is known for her compassionate and inclusive leadership style. She responded to the Christchurch mosque shootings with empathy and unity, fostering a sense of national solidarity. Ardern's leadership highlights the importance of compassion and inclusivity in building strong, resilient communities.

The Power of Women's Leadership

Women who overcome personal and societal challenges often emerge as powerful leaders. A woman sitting in her house, dealing with injustice, can become a beacon of hope and strength for millions. Her journey from overcoming personal struggles to leading others demonstrates the transformative power of resilience and determination.

Case Study: Dr. Rani Bang, Social Reformer and Public Health Advocate

Dr. Rani Bang's story is one of extraordinary bravery and commitment to improving public health in some of India's most underserved areas. Alongside her husband, Dr. Abhay Bang, she has been a pioneering force in bringing healthcare to the tribal regions of Maharashtra through their organization, SEARCH (Society for Education, Action, and Research in Community Health).

In the late 1980s, Dr. Rani Bang and her husband moved to the remote district of Gadchiroli, a region plagued by poverty, lack of infrastructure, and limited access to healthcare. Despite the immense challenges, including resistance from local communities and the difficulties of working in such a remote area, Dr. Bang's bravery and determination led her to establish a healthcare model that was both innovative and deeply empathetic.

Dr. Bang's work in maternal and child health, particularly her research on women's reproductive health, challenged long-held taboos and brought critical issues to the forefront of public health in India. Her bravery in confronting these sensitive topics and advocating for change in a conservative society has saved countless lives and transformed the health landscape of the region.

Dr. Rani Bang's leadership is a powerful example of how courage, integrity, and empathy can come together to drive social change. Her story inspires not only those in the field of public health but also anyone committed to making a difference in the face of adversity.

Wangari Maathai: Environmental and Political Activist: Wangari Maathai, the first African woman to receive the Nobel Peace Prize, faced significant opposition in her fight for environmental conservation and women's rights in Kenya. Despite numerous challenges, Maathai's commitment to justice and sustainability led to the establishment of the Green Belt Movement, which has planted millions of trees and empowered women across Africa.

Case Study: Falguni Nayar, Founder and CEO of Nykaa

Falguni Nayar's leadership journey is a testament to the power of vision, resilience, and integrity. After a successful career in investment banking, Falguni took a bold step at the age of 50, venturing into the beauty and wellness industry by founding Nykaa, one of India's leading e-commerce platforms for beauty products. Despite entering a highly competitive market dominated by global giants, Falguni's unwavering commitment to integrity and her deep understanding of the Indian consumer propelled Nykaa to become a household name.

Falguni's leadership is characterized by her ethical approach to business and her dedication to empowering women. Under her guidance, Nykaa has built a reputation for transparency and quality, earning the trust of millions of customers. She has also been a vocal advocate for women's entrepreneurship, demonstrating that integrity in leadership is not only about achieving success but also about uplifting others along the way.

Falguni Nayar's story is a powerful example of how integrity and resilience can drive business success and inspire a new generation of women leaders in India and beyond.

Personal Commitment to an Equal World

Injustice is a wound to the fabric of our shared humanity—a wound that I cannot, and will not, turn away from. The call to overcome it is not just an echo in the distance but a resonant beat within my heart, compelling me to act. My commitment to an equal world is not a mere abstract ideal; it is the compass that guides every decision, every action, and every word I speak.

Equality is not just about leveling the playing field; it is about recognizing the inherent dignity and worth of every individual, regardless of their background, gender, race, or circumstance. This commitment requires more than just conversations around the dinner table or well-meaning discussions in boardrooms. It demands courage—the courage to confront biases, the courage to challenge the status quo, and the courage to advocate for those who cannot advocate for themselves.

In a world where discrimination is often entrenched in the systems we navigate daily, it becomes our collective responsibility to dismantle these barriers. My commitment to an equal world is a pledge to stand against injustice wherever it is found, to amplify voices that have been silenced, and to ensure that the policies we champion are not just inclusive in name but in practice.

This journey towards equality is not easy, nor is it quick. It is fraught with resistance and setbacks. Yet, it is in these moments of struggle that our resolve is tested and strengthened. The fight for equality is a marathon, not a sprint—one that we must run with perseverance, guided by the belief that a just and equal world is not just a dream but a necessity.

Through my work, I seek to create spaces where everyone has the opportunity to thrive, where diversity is not just tolerated but celebrated, and where the richness of our differences enhances rather than divides us. My commitment is to an equal world—one where justice is not a privilege for the few but a right for all.

This commitment shapes not only who I am but also the legacy I hope to leave behind. It is my personal pledge to stand in solidarity with the marginalized, to be a voice of reason and compassion in the face of inequality, and to never lose sight of the vision of a world where every person, no matter who they are, can stand tall with dignity and pride.

Building a Roadmap for Cultural Leadership

1. **Understand and Respect Diversity**: Take the time to learn about different cultures, backgrounds, and perspectives. Respect and value these differences.

2. **Promote Inclusive Practices**: Implement policies and practices that promote inclusivity, such as flexible work arrangements, diversity training, and mentorship programs.

3. **Challenge Biases and Stereotypes**: Actively challenge biases and stereotypes in the workplace. Encourage open discussions and create a safe space for all voices to be heard.

4. **Support Diverse Leadership**: Advocate for policies that support diverse leadership, such as equal pay, maternity leave, and childcare facilities. Mentor and support individuals from underrepresented groups in their professional journeys.

5. **Lead by Example**: Demonstrate your commitment to diversity and inclusion through your actions. Be a role model for others to follow.

Conclusion

Cultural leadership is about more than just leading diverse teams; it is about creating a world where everyone has the opportunity to succeed. By embracing diversity and championing equality, we can build stronger, more innovative organisations and communities.

As leaders, we have a responsibility to challenge injustice and advocate for an equal world. Whether it is supporting women in leadership, promoting inclusive practices, or challenging biases, our actions can create lasting change.

In the words of Ruth Bader Ginsburg, "Fight for the things that you care about, but do it in a way that will lead others to join you." Let this be our guiding principle as we strive to be cultural leaders who embrace diversity and champion equality. By doing so, we can create a world where everyone has the opportunity to thrive.

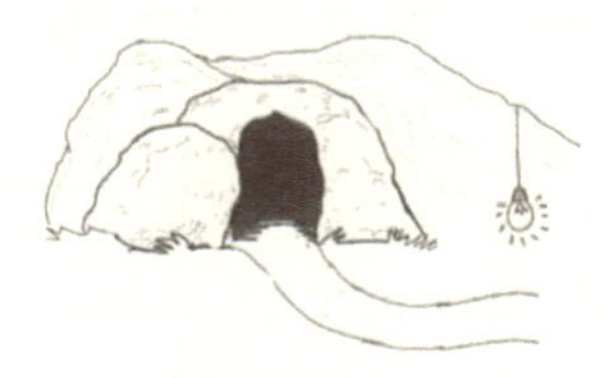

<h1 style="text-align:center">Chapter Twenty</h1>

From Shadows to Light: The Power of Gratitude in Personal Growth

As we near the end of this journey through leadership, resilience, and diversity, it is essential to focus on personal growth. Personal growth is not just about achieving goals; it's about continuously evolving, learning, and transforming ourselves. It is a journey from the shadows of self-doubt, failure, and limitations to the light of self-awareness, resilience, and empowerment. This chapter delves into the profound impact of personal growth and how embracing this journey, with a special emphasis on gratitude, can make us better leaders and individuals.

The Foundations of Personal Growth

1. **Self-Awareness and Understanding**
   Personal growth begins with self-awareness and understanding. This involves recognizing our strengths and weaknesses, understanding our emotions, and knowing our values. Self-

awareness is the foundation upon which we build our ability to grow and lead effectively.

2. **Learning from Failure**

Failure is a critical component of personal growth. Leaders like Roger Federer and Steve Jobs have shown that failure is not a setback, but a stepping stone to success. Embracing failure, analyzing our mistakes, and learning from them builds resilience and develops a growth mindset.

3. **Cultivating Empathy, Integrity, and Gratitude**

Empathy, integrity, and gratitude are essential for personal and professional growth. Leaders like Kiran Mazumdar-Shaw and Tim Cook embody these values, demonstrating that empathy allows us to connect with others, integrity ensures we stay true to our principles, and gratitude fosters a positive, appreciative mindset that enhances our leadership effectiveness.

4. **Overcoming Insecurity and Jealousy**

Insecurity and jealousy can hinder personal growth. These emotions stem from fear and self-doubt. Overcoming them requires self-awareness and self-compassion, allowing us to transform insecurity into confidence and jealousy into inspiration.

5. **Embracing Diversity and Inclusion**

Embracing diversity enriches our lives and fosters innovation and growth. Leaders like Sundar Pichai and Jacinda Ardern show that promoting inclusivity and challenging biases create environments where everyone can thrive.

6. **Fighting Injustice and Advocating Equality**

Fighting against injustice and advocating for equality are crucial for societal and personal growth. Leaders like Malala Yousafzai and Wangari Maathai inspire us to confront challenges and use them as catalysts for change.

7. **Building Resilience**

    Resilience is the ability to bounce back from setbacks and adapt to change. It is a vital component of personal growth, enabling us to face challenges head-on and emerge stronger.

8. **The Power of Gratitude in Personal Growth**

    Gratitude in leadership is more than a mere practice—it is a transformative mindset that fosters resilience, builds stronger relationships, and enhances our ability to lead with empathy and integrity. It allows leaders to recognize and appreciate the contributions of others, creating an environment of mutual respect and motivation. Two people in my life have been instrumental in teaching me the power of gratitude: Brijesh and Pooja.

Brijesh - The Student Who Became a Teacher

Gratitude is a fundamental aspect of leadership, often overlooked in the pursuit of success. It was Brijesh, a former student, who taught me the profound importance of gratitude and how to incorporate it into my daily leadership practice.

When Brijesh first started studying with me, he was eager to learn and full of enthusiasm. He approached every task with a positive attitude and a willingness to help others. Despite the challenges he faced, Brijesh always expressed gratitude for every opportunity and experience, no matter how small. His attitude was contagious, and it made me realize the power of gratitude in fostering a positive and productive environment.

Through Brijesh, I learned that gratitude is not just about saying "thank you" but about recognizing the value in every experience and the efforts of those around us. In leadership, this recognition is crucial—it helps build a culture of appreciation where team members feel valued and motivated to contribute their best.

Brijesh's ability to find joy and appreciation in every situation inspired me to adopt a similar approach. By practicing gratitude, I noticed a shift in my leadership style. I became more mindful of my team's contributions, more aware of the support I received, and more committed to fostering an environment where everyone's efforts were acknowledged.

This approach to leadership not only improved the morale of my team but also led to increased productivity and innovation. Gratitude, as Brijesh demonstrated, is not just a feel-good emotion; it's a powerful tool that can transform relationships, enhance collaboration, and build a stronger, more cohesive team. Brijesh's influence has been a testament to the idea that sometimes, our greatest teachers come from unexpected places, and the lessons they impart can have a lasting impact on how we lead.

Pooja: The Smile That Teaches Gratitude

If Brijesh taught me the power of gratitude in practice, Pooja showed me the beauty of gratitude in the everyday moments of life. Pooja is the friend who always checks up on me, who is sensitive to my moods, and who, no matter what life throws her way, always has a smile on her face. Her unwavering positivity and concern for others have had a profound impact on my understanding of gratitude and its role in leadership.

There was a time when I was particularly stressed about a project, and my frustration was evident to those around me. Pooja, with her usual grace and warmth, noticed my mood immediately. Instead of asking directly about the project, she invited me for a cup of coffee, something she often does when she senses I need a break. As we sat down, she began talking about the little things in life she was grateful for—her morning walk, the laughter she shared with her family, the support of friends.

As she spoke, I realized that she wasn't just trying to distract me from my worries; she was gently guiding me to see the positive side of life, even in stressful times. Her simple, heartfelt words reminded me of the value of gratitude, not just as a practice, but as a way of viewing the world. This shift in perspective was crucial, especially in leadership, where the pressures can sometimes overshadow the small joys that keep us grounded.

Pooja's ability to find joy in the small, everyday moments made me realize that gratitude is a powerful tool in leadership. It helps us stay connected to our teams, fosters a sense of community, and reminds us to appreciate the contributions of others, even during challenging times. That day, I walked away not just feeling lighter, but with a renewed sense of appreciation for the people and experiences in my life. Pooja's smile, her kind words, and her ability to turn even the toughest day into something positive reminded me that gratitude is not just about the big things; it's about appreciating the little things that make life beautiful.

In leadership, this lesson is invaluable. By practicing gratitude, leaders can create a more positive work environment, build stronger relationships with their teams, and foster a culture of mutual respect and appreciation. Pooja's influence helped me understand that gratitude is a cornerstone of effective leadership, and it's a practice that can transform not only our perspective but also the way we lead others.

Practical Steps for Personal Growth

The Foundations of Personal Growth Through Gratitude

1. **Self-Awareness and Understanding**
   Personal growth begins with self-awareness and understanding, and gratitude plays a crucial role in this process. When we practice gratitude, we become more aware of the positive aspects of our lives and the people who contribute to our success. This awareness helps us understand our strengths and weaknesses, and it guides us toward continuous self-improvement.

2. **Learning from Failure**
   Failure is a critical component of personal growth, but it can be challenging to view setbacks as opportunities. Gratitude helps us reframe failure, allowing us to see the lessons it offers rather than simply the pain it causes. Leaders like J.K. Rowling, who faced numerous rejections before Harry Potter became a global phenomenon, have shown that gratitude for the lessons learned from failure can propel us toward success.

3. **Cultivating Empathy, Integrity, and Gratitude**

   Empathy, integrity, and gratitude are essential for personal and professional growth. Leaders like Satya Nadella, CEO of Microsoft, have demonstrated how these values can transform an organization. Nadella's empathetic leadership style, combined with his commitment to integrity and a culture of gratitude, has revitalized Microsoft and fostered innovation and collaboration. Gratitude allows leaders to appreciate the efforts of their teams, creating a positive work environment where integrity and empathy thrive.

4. **Overcoming Insecurity and Jealousy**

   Insecurity and jealousy can hinder personal growth. These emotions often stem from fear and self-doubt. By practicing gratitude, we can shift our focus from what we lack to what we have, transforming insecurity into confidence and jealousy into inspiration. Consider the example of Arianna Huffington, who, after experiencing burnout, learned to appreciate the small moments of peace and joy in her life. Her practice of gratitude helped her overcome insecurities and inspired her to launch Thrive Global, an organization focused on well-being and productivity.

5. **Embracing Diversity and Inclusion**

   Embracing diversity enriches our lives and fosters innovation and growth. Leaders like Indra Nooyi, former CEO of PepsiCo, have shown that gratitude for diverse perspectives can lead to better decision-making and a more inclusive work environment. Nooyi's appreciation for the unique contributions of each team member helped create a culture where everyone felt valued and empowered to share their ideas.

6. **Fighting Injustice and Advocating Equality**

   Fighting against injustice and advocating for equality are crucial for societal and personal growth. Leaders like Nelson Mandela found strength in gratitude, even during his years of imprisonment. Mandela's gratitude for the support of his fellow prisoners and the lessons he learned during his struggle for freedom fueled his lifelong commitment to justice and equality. His story inspires us to confront challenges with a grateful heart, using them as catalysts for positive change.

7. **Building Resilience**

   Resilience is the ability to bounce back from setbacks and adapt to change. It is a vital component of personal growth, enabling us to face challenges head-on and emerge stronger. Oprah Winfrey, a leader in media and philanthropy, credits much of her resilience to her practice of gratitude. Despite facing numerous adversities, Oprah's focus on gratitude has allowed her to maintain a positive outlook and build a successful, impactful career.

Examples of Gratitude in Leadership

Richard Branson is known for his adventurous spirit and innovative leadership style, but at the heart of his success is a deep sense of gratitude. Branson often speaks about the importance of showing appreciation to his employees, customers, and even his competitors. He believes that gratitude fosters a positive company culture, encourages creativity, and drives long-term success. One of Branson's practices is writing handwritten thank-you notes to employees who go above and beyond, a simple yet powerful gesture that has contributed to the strong, loyal culture within the Virgin Group. Branson's approach to leadership reminds us that gratitude is not only about recognizing big achievements but also about appreciating the small, everyday contributions that make success possible.

How Leadership Merges Into Life: The Transformative Power of Gratitude

Leadership is not confined to the boardroom or the workplace; it permeates every aspect of our lives. The values and practices we cultivate as leaders inevitably influence how we interact with our families, friends, and communities. Gratitude, in particular, is a value that seamlessly integrates leadership with life, transforming not only our professional relationships but also our personal connections.

1. **Gratitude Strengthens Relationships**

   In leadership, gratitude fosters stronger, more positive relationships with team members. This principle applies equally to our personal lives. By practicing gratitude with our loved ones, we build deeper, more meaningful connections. Just as a leader's appreciation can motivate and inspire a team, expressing gratitude in our personal relationships can strengthen bonds and create a supportive, loving environment.

2. **Gratitude Enhances Well-Being**

   Leaders who practice gratitude often report higher levels of satisfaction and well-being, both personally and professionally. This is because gratitude shifts our focus from what we lack to what we have, promoting a positive mindset. In life, this practice can reduce stress, improve mental health, and lead to greater overall happiness. Whether in moments of success or during challenging times, gratitude helps us maintain perspective and find joy in the journey.

3. **Gratitude Encourages a Growth Mindset**

    In leadership, gratitude encourages a growth mindset by helping us see challenges as opportunities for learning and improvement. This mindset is equally valuable in life. When we approach personal challenges with gratitude, we are more likely to embrace change, seek out new experiences, and continuously evolve. Gratitude keeps us open to growth, enabling us to become better leaders, partners, and individuals.

4. **Gratitude Cultivates Resilience**

    Resilience is a critical trait in both leadership and life. Practicing gratitude builds resilience by helping us focus on the positive aspects of our experiences, even during difficult times. By acknowledging and appreciating the support we receive from others, we strengthen our ability to bounce back from setbacks. This resilience is not only beneficial in our careers but also in our personal lives, where challenges often test our strength and resolve.

Conclusion: The Journey from Shadows to Light

The journey from shadows to light is one of continuous personal growth. By embracing failures, cultivating empathy, integrity, and gratitude, championing diversity and inclusion, and building resilience, we become better leaders and individuals. Personal growth is a lifelong process that requires us to strive to be the best versions of ourselves, inspiring others and making a positive impact on the world.

Gratitude, as I have learned from Brijesh and Pooja, is a powerful force that not only enhances our leadership but also enriches our lives. It teaches us to appreciate the journey, to value the contributions of others, and to find joy in the small moments that make life meaningful. As leaders, let us carry forward the lessons of gratitude, using them to light our path from shadows to light, guiding us to personal growth and fulfillment.

In the words of Nelson Mandela, "I never lose. I either win or learn." Let this be our guiding principle as we continue on our journey from shadows to light, embracing every experience and opportunity for growth, and leading with gratitude and integrity.

Chapter Twenty One

The Future of Leadership: Evolving Dynamics

As we conclude this journey through leadership, resilience, and diversity, it is essential to look forward and consider the future of leadership. The landscape of leadership has evolved significantly over the years and will continue to change in response to the dynamic world we live in. This chapter explores how leadership has transformed, how it will keep evolving, and how we can stay present while preparing for an uncertain future. By reflecting on the lessons learned and envisioning the path ahead, we aim to inspire a new generation of leaders who are equipped to navigate the complexities of the modern world.

The Evolution of Leadership

1. **Historical Context: From Authority to Empowerment**
   Leadership has always been shaped by the context in which it operates. Traditional leadership was often hierarchical and

authoritarian, characterized by top-down decision-making with limited input from lower levels of the organization. Leaders were seen as the ultimate authority figures, whose word was law, and whose power was rarely questioned.

2. **Transformational Leadership: Inspiring Change**

   As societies and organizations became more complex, a new style of leadership emerged—transformational leadership. This approach focuses on inspiring and motivating employees, fostering a shared vision, and empowering others to achieve their fullest potential. Leaders like Nelson Mandela and Mahatma Gandhi exemplified this approach, using their influence to drive significant social and political change by connecting deeply with the values and aspirations of those they led.

3. **Inclusive Leadership: Embracing Diversity**

   In recent years, the importance of diversity and inclusion in leadership has gained recognition. Inclusive leadership values diverse perspectives and creates environments where everyone feels valued and respected. Leaders like Jacinda Ardern and Tim Cook demonstrate the power of inclusivity in driving success. Their leadership styles show that by embracing different viewpoints and fostering a sense of belonging, leaders can create more innovative, resilient, and effective organizations.

The Future of Leadership: Navigating the Unknown

1. **Technological Advancements: Embracing Innovation**

   Technological advancements, such as artificial intelligence, automation, and big data, are transforming the way we work and lead. Future leaders must embrace these technologies to drive innovation and efficiency while being mindful of their ethical implications. The challenge lies in balancing technological progress with human values, ensuring that the benefits of innovation are shared equitably and sustainably.

2. **Globalization: Leading in a Connected World**

   Globalization has connected the world like never before, creating both opportunities and challenges for leaders. Navigating cultural differences, managing diverse teams, and addressing global issues will be essential for future leaders. As the world becomes increasingly interconnected, leaders must cultivate cultural intelligence, empathy, and adaptability to lead effectively across borders and disciplines.

3. **Agile and Resilient Organizations: Adapting to Change**

   The pace of change in today's world requires leaders to build agile and resilient organizations. This involves fostering a culture of continuous learning, encouraging innovation, and empowering employees to take initiative. Agile leaders are those who can pivot quickly in response to new information, who view challenges as opportunities for growth, and who inspire their teams to embrace change rather than fear it.

4. **Mental Health and Well-being: Prioritizing People**

   The future of leadership will place a greater emphasis on mental health and well-being. Leaders must create supportive environments where employees feel safe to express their concerns and seek help. Prioritizing well-being enhances productivity and fosters a more engaged and loyal workforce. As mental health becomes a more central concern in the workplace, leaders will need to be compassionate, understanding, and proactive in addressing the well-being of their teams.

Staying Present While Preparing for the Future

1. **Mindfulness: Leading with Clarity and Purpose**

   Mindfulness helps leaders stay present and focused in the face of uncertainty. Practicing mindfulness enhances self-awareness, reduces stress, and improves decision-making. It involves taking the time to reflect, being present in the moment, and cultivating gratitude for the journey. Mindful leaders are those who lead with intention, who are attuned to the needs of their teams, and who make decisions that align with their core values.

2. **Scenario Planning: Preparing for Multiple Futures**

   Scenario planning is a strategic tool that helps leaders prepare for an uncertain future. By envisioning different possible futures and developing strategies for each, leaders can adapt to unexpected changes. This proactive approach enables leaders to remain flexible and resilient, ensuring that they are prepared for a range of potential outcomes.

3. **Encouraging Innovation: Fostering a Culture of Creativity**

   Innovation is crucial for staying relevant in a rapidly changing world. Leaders must create environments where experimentation is encouraged, and failure is seen as a learning opportunity. By fostering a culture of creativity, leaders can drive continuous improvement and inspire their teams to push the boundaries of what is possible.

Connecting the Dots: A Roadmap to Leadership and Personal Growth

Reflecting on the journey through this book, each chapter has provided valuable insights and lessons that build a comprehensive roadmap for leadership and personal growth. Here's how these themes come together to shape the future of leadership:

1. **The Many Faces of Leadership:** This chapter explored the diverse styles of leadership and how adaptability is key to being an effective leader. Understanding that leadership is not one-size-fits-all allows leaders to navigate various challenges and environments successfully.

2. **The Human Side of Leadership:** Here, we delved into the importance of empathy and connection in leadership. Recognizing the human aspects of those we lead fosters trust and enhances relationships, making leaders more relatable and effective.

3. **The Art of Listening:** Effective leadership begins with the ability to listen. This chapter emphasized the power of active listening in building trust, understanding, and collaboration within teams.

4. **The Heartbeat of Leadership:** This chapter focused on passion and commitment as the driving forces behind successful leadership. Leaders who are passionate about their mission inspire and motivate others to achieve great things.

5. **Ambition: The Fire and the Burn:** Ambition is a double-edged sword—it can drive success but also lead to burnout if not managed carefully. This chapter examined how leaders can harness ambition while maintaining balance.

6. **The Shadow of Insecurity:** Insecurity can be a significant barrier to effective leadership. This chapter discussed how overcoming personal insecurities is crucial for leaders to build confidence and inspire others.

7. **The Power of Vulnerability:** Vulnerability is often seen as a weakness, but this chapter explored how embracing vulnerability can actually strengthen leadership by fostering authenticity and deeper connections.

8. **The Loneliness of Leadership:** Leadership can be isolating, and this chapter addressed the emotional challenges leaders face when they feel alone in their decisions and responsibilities.

9. **The Impact of Power:** Power has a profound influence on behavior and decision-making. This chapter examined how leaders can wield power responsibly and the effects it can have on those they lead.

10. **The Dual Nature of Power:** Power can be both constructive and destructive, depending on how it is used. This chapter explored the fine line leaders must walk to ensure their power is a force for good.

11. **Styles of Leadership: Adapting to Thrive:** This chapter highlighted the importance of adapting leadership styles to different situations and challenges, showing how flexibility is vital to thriving in leadership roles.

12. **Confessions of a Leader:** A deeply personal chapter, this explored the challenges and inner conflicts leaders face, offering a candid look at the pressures of leadership.

13. **Power and Responsibility: A Delicate Balance:** Balancing power with responsibility is essential for ethical leadership. This chapter discussed the importance of accountability and the ethical use of power.

14. **Abuse of Power: The Dark Path:** Ethical conduct is crucial to maintaining trust and integrity. This chapter warned of the

dangers of power abuse and the consequences it can have on leaders and their organizations.

15. **Transforming Through True Mentorship:** Mentorship plays a pivotal role in leadership development. This chapter explored how being both a mentor and a mentee can transform and elevate leadership practices.

16. **Leadership in Crisis: Navigating Storms:** Effective crisis management is a hallmark of great leadership. This chapter provided insights into how leaders can navigate crises with composure, transparency, and strength.

17. **Empathy and Integrity: The Core of Leadership:** These values are the foundation of sustainable leadership. This chapter reinforced how empathy and integrity build trust, inspire loyalty, and sustain long-term success.

18. **Building Resilience: Lessons from Failure:** Failure is an inevitable part of the leadership journey, but it is also a powerful teacher. This chapter shared lessons on how leaders can build resilience through setbacks and failures.

19. **Cultural Leadership: Embracing Diversity:** Embracing diversity and promoting inclusion are essential for modern leadership. This chapter emphasized the importance of valuing diverse perspectives and creating environments where everyone feels respected and valued.

20. **From Shadows to Light: The Power of Gratitude in Personal Growth:** Personal growth is a journey from self-doubt to empowerment, and gratitude is the guiding light. This chapter explored how gratitude can transform leadership, foster resilience, and deepen connections with others.

21. **The Future of Leadership: Evolving Dynamics:** As we look to the future, we must embrace change, adapt to new

realities, and lead with purpose and integrity. This chapter considered how leadership is evolving and what leaders must do to stay effective in a rapidly changing world.

The Moral of Our Story: Leadership for a New Era

Leadership is not about holding power over others; it is about empowering others to achieve their fullest potential. It is about embracing diversity, fostering inclusion, and leading with empathy and integrity. As we move forward, let us remember that the true measure of a leader lies not in the power they wield, but in the lives they touch, the integrity they uphold, and the legacy they leave behind.

1. **Embrace Failure as a Stepping Stone:** Failure is not the end, but a beginning. Embrace it, learn from it, and use it as a stepping stone to greater success.
2. **Lead with Empathy and Integrity:** Empathy and integrity are the cornerstones of effective leadership. They build trust, inspire others, and create a lasting impact.
3. **Champion Diversity and Inclusion:** Diversity and inclusion are not just buzzwords; they are essential for fostering innovation and driving success in a globalized world.
4. **Build Resilience:** Resilience is crucial for navigating the challenges and uncertainties of leadership. It's what enables us to bounce back, adapt, and keep moving forward.

Defining Your Leadership Legacy

A leadership legacy is the enduring impact a leader has on their organization, industry, or community. It is the sum of the changes, values, and improvements that persist long after the leader has moved on. Creating a lasting positive impact requires intentionality and a focus on long-term goals.

Strategies for Creating a Lasting Positive Impact:

1. **Mentorship and Development:** Invest in the growth and development of others. Mentor future leaders and provide opportunities for them to learn and grow.
2. **Fostering a Positive Culture:** Build and sustain a positive organizational culture that promotes ethical behavior, collaboration, and innovation.
3. **Sustainable Practices:** Implement sustainable practices that ensure long-term success and environmental responsibility.
4. **Championing Inclusivity:** Advocate for diversity and inclusion, ensuring that all voices are heard and valued.
5. **Documenting Wisdom:** Share your knowledge and experiences through writing, speaking, and teaching to inspire and guide future leaders.

Examples of Leaders with Enduring Legacies:

- **Mahatma Gandhi:** Gandhi's commitment to non-violence and social justice has left an indelible mark on the world. His principles continue to inspire movements for peace and equality.
- **Steve Jobs:** Steve Jobs' vision and innovation transformed the technology industry. His legacy lives on through Apple's continued success and influence.

Personal Reflections: The Legacy I Aspire to Leave

Reflecting on my own journey, I strive to leave a legacy of empowerment, integrity, and positive change. I hope to be remembered not just for my achievements, but for the values I upheld and the lives I impacted. One of my proudest moments came when a former team member reached out years later to thank me for the mentorship and support that had helped shape their career. Knowing that I had made a positive impact on their life reaffirmed my commitment to leading with integrity and compassion.

Building a Roadmap for Your Leadership Legacy:

1. **Identify Core Values:** Determine the values you want to be remembered for.
2. **Set Long-Term Goals:** Define the lasting impact you want to have.
3. **Invest in Others:** Focus on developing and empowering those around you.
4. **Promote Sustainability:** Implement practices that ensure long-term success and well-being.
5. **Document Your Journey:** Share your insights and experiences to guide future leaders.

Leading with Purpose: The Legacy of Leadership

The legacy of leadership is about more than just the results you achieve; it is about the positive impact you make on the world. By leading with purpose, integrity, and compassion, we can create a lasting legacy that inspires and empowers future generations.

Conclusion: The Future of Leadership

The future of leadership is dynamic and ever-evolving. To navigate this future successfully, we must stay grounded in the present, embrace change, and continuously strive for personal and professional growth. The lessons learned throughout this journey provide the foundation for becoming effective, compassionate, and visionary leaders.

As we move forward, let us remember that leadership is about more than just achieving success; it is about making a positive impact on the world. It is about inspiring and empowering others, fostering a culture of inclusion and innovation, and leading with purpose and integrity.

In the words of John Quincy Adams, "If your actions inspire others to dream more, learn more, do more, and become more, you are a leader." Let this be our guiding principle as we continue to evolve and lead in an ever-changing world. Embrace every challenge, every opportunity, and every moment as a chance to grow and make a difference. By doing so, we can create a brighter and more inclusive future for all.

As we conclude this journey, remember that leadership is not just about wielding power; it is about making a lasting, positive impact. It is about the lives we touch, the values we uphold, and the legacy we leave behind. Lead with love, lead with light, and let your actions be the beacon that guides others on their journey from shadows to light.

Poetic Reflection: Leadership's Legacy

In the quiet echoes of the night,
Where dreams and fears entwine,
Leadership's torch burns ever bright,
A journey vast, both yours and mine.

Through valleys deep and mountains tall,
We faced the storms, we heeded the call.
With hearts of courage and minds so keen,
In every shadow, a light was seen.

Empathy, the gentle thread,
Woven through our path ahead.
In every trial, a lesson learned,
In every heart, a fire burned.

With friends beside, who spoke the truth,
Their wisdom guided in times of ruth.
Mentors' hands, so firm, so kind,
Shaping vision, sharpening mind.

Ambition's fire, both fierce and warm,
A guiding star in every storm.
Yet, balanced with a humble heart,
It forged a legacy set apart.

Insecurity, the hidden foe,
In silent whispers, it would sow,
Seeds of doubt, yet in their place,
We found our strength, our saving grace.

Power wielded with integrity,
Became a force of unity.
In every choice, with care, we tread,
Aware of those we've gently led.

As we close this book, reflect and see,
The essence of leadership, in you, in me.
It's not in titles, but in deeds,
In hearts that serve, in minds that lead.

So here's to the journey, the paths we pave,
To the souls we touch, the lives we save.
With every step, in truth, in might,
We lead with love, we lead with light.

–Nirbhay Vassa

Reflections and Aspirations

As I stand at the close of this journey, I am filled with profound gratitude and a sense of accomplishment that words can barely capture. Writing "Confessions of Power" has been more than just a creative endeavor—it has been a transformative odyssey, one that has allowed me to confront my own truths, celebrate my victories, and learn from the moments that tested the very core of my leadership.

This book is not just a collection of experiences; it is a reflection of the path we all walk as leaders. It is about the scars we bear from battles fought, the lessons we glean from mentors and peers, and the wisdom that only failure can bestow. My deepest hope is that these stories resonate with you, serving as both a mirror and a compass as you forge your own leadership journey.

Leadership, I have learned, is not a static destination but a dynamic, ever-evolving process. It demands relentless self-reflection, the humility to learn, and the audacity to adapt in the face of change. As I continue to evolve, I am more committed than ever to leading with integrity, with empathy, and with an unwavering sense of purpose. I am inspired not only by the great leaders of the past but by the emerging voices of the future—those who will redefine the contours of leadership with their unique perspectives and indomitable spirit.

Looking ahead, my aspirations extend beyond personal achievement. I am dedicated to the mission of mentoring and empowering others, of cultivating environments where every individual has the opportunity to thrive. My passion lies in creating spaces where diversity of thought is not just welcomed but celebrated, where every voice is heard, and every contribution is valued.

To you, my readers, I offer my heartfelt thanks. Your engagement with this book breathes life into its pages, and for that, I am deeply grateful. "Confessions of Power" is as much your journey as it is mine. I hope that within these pages, you have found the insights and inspiration needed to lead with heart, conviction, and a profound sense of responsibility.

As we stand at the threshold of the future, I urge you to embrace the unknown with courage and curiosity. Leadership is not about the power we hold; it is about the power we give others to succeed. It is about building bridges, fostering trust, and guiding with a vision that transcends the self.

In the spirit of giving back, I want to share that all the proceeds from this book will go towards causes close to my heart: women empowerment, education, and providing food for the underprivileged. These causes resonate deeply with me, and I am committed to making a difference, however small. There are moments that stay with me—the gratitude in a mother's eyes as she learns a new skill to support her family, the joy of children receiving the education they deserve, and the relief on the faces of those who receive a warm meal they might otherwise have gone without. These experiences have not only enriched the lives of others but have also made me feel more complete.

I know that my contributions are just a small drop in the ocean, but I believe in the ripple effect of kindness. Giving back is not just a duty; it's a way to connect with the humanity we all share.

Thank you for walking this path with me. May your vulnerabilities be your strength, your convictions your compass, and the stories of your journey the beacon that lights the way for others.

References and Inspirations

As a first-time author, I owe a debt of gratitude to the many books, authors, and leaders who have inspired me throughout this journey. Here is a heartfelt acknowledgement of the sources that influenced "Confessions of Power":

"Good to Great" by Jim Collins - For teaching me the importance of disciplined thought and action.

"Leaders Eat Last" by Simon Sinek - For highlighting the value of empathy and trust in leadership.

"The Art of War" by Sun Tzu - For strategic insights that have stood the test of time.

"Steve Jobs" by Walter Isaacson - For an in-depth look at visionary leadership and innovation.

"Long Walk to Freedom" by Nelson Mandela - For lessons in resilience, forgiveness, and transformative leadership.

"The Seven Habits of Highly Effective People" by Stephen Covey - For timeless principles that guide personal and professional growth.

"Playing It My Way" by Sachin Tendulkar - For inspiration from the life of a cricketing legend.

"Leading" by Alex Ferguson - For insights into leadership from one of football's greatest managers.

"Autobiography of a Yogi" by Paramahansa Yogananda - For spiritual guidance and the pursuit of inner peace.

"Batman: The Dark Knight Returns" by Frank Miller - For the enduring lessons in resilience and justice from my favourite superhero.

"Start with Why" by Simon Sinek - For emphasizing the importance of purpose in leadership.

"Dare to Lead" by Brené Brown - For insights into the power of vulnerability and courage in leadership.

"Emotional Intelligence" by Daniel Goleman - For exploring the critical role of emotional intelligence in effective leadership.

"Lean In" by Sheryl Sandberg - For advocating gender equality and resilience in the workplace.

"Mindfulness in Plain English" by Bhante Henepola Gunaratana - For practical guidance on mindfulness and its application in leadership.

These books, along with countless articles, quotes, and conversations, have shaped my understanding of leadership and influenced the writing of this book. I am grateful for the wisdom and inspiration they have provided, and I hope to pay it forward by sharing my own experiences and insights with you.

Echoes of Leadership: Reflections from Those Who Followed

A Tribute to Leadership: Rahul's Reflections on Nirbhay

In my five-year journey with Nirbhay, I've witnessed firsthand the essence of true leadership. Nirbhay is a leader who can guide, inspire, and motivate individuals to achieve feats they never thought possible. He is a people person who draws energy from connecting with others, and this connection forms the foundation of his leadership.

The major leadership skills I've learned from him encompass empathy, networking, communication, and fearless vision. Nirbhay embodies passion, accountability, assertiveness, creativity, and adaptability to change. His ability to handle difficult situations with composure is particularly noteworthy.

Nirbhay has instilled in me the understanding that anyone can be a leader if they possess vision, passion, and accountability. He taught me to treat my work with the same dedication and ownership as a promoter or entrepreneur, which builds trust with colleagues, clients, and team members alike. This mindset has been pivotal in Nirbhay's remarkable rise within the organisation to Group CFO and Whole-Time Director.

Observing and learning from Nirbhay has significantly enhanced my professional growth. Transitioning from an individual contributor to a team leader has been a remarkable journey, marked by continuous learning and development. When faced with challenging situations, I often find myself asking, "What would Nirbhay do?" This simple reflection invariably leads to viable solutions.

The impact of a leader like Nirbhay extends far beyond individual growth. He has groomed and mentored many, leaving a lasting impression on all who have had the privilege of learning from him. His wisdom and guidance have shaped not only my career, but also the careers of many others.

I consider myself fortunate to have a mentor and leader like Nirbhay. His influence has been instrumental in my development, and for that, I am profoundly grateful. Thank you, Nirbhay, for all the guidance and wisdom you have imparted.

From Mentorship to Fatherhood – Aditya's heartfelt note

I am immensely grateful to my mentor, Nirbhay sir, who has been a guiding star and a fatherly figure in my life. His profound expertise in our field has been a cornerstone of my career advancement, providing me with invaluable advice and insights that have propelled me forward. Beyond his professional acumen, he has shown unwavering dedication to my well-being, offering steadfast encouragement during challenging times and celebrating my achievements with genuine pride.

There have been countless moments when his support transcended the professional realm, becoming a source of fatherly guidance that ensured my aspirations remained bright. His mentorship has not only charted the course of my career but has also profoundly influenced my personal growth. He created a nurturing environment where I could thrive, imparting life lessons that have indelibly shaped my perspective on both work and life.

His guidance, embodying both mentorship and paternal care, has been instrumental in moulding me into the professional and individual I am today. His saying, "Hum apni tayari behetar logo ke saath karte hai," (We prepare ourselves with wiser examples in mind), has become ingrained in my DNA, inspiring me daily to strive for excellence and give my utmost effort.

To the Man Who Shaped My Mind – Kind words from Sheriar

A mentor holds the same influence as parents do over their children growing up. For the past four years, I have spent ten hours a day absorbing everything you have to teach. Through these experiences, I have learned more than any book or educational degree could offer.

You have given me the ability to face life head-on, to stand in the face of adversity and say, "Come get me." The valuable lessons and accelerated growth you provided have been invaluable. A mentor's job is to identify potential, exploit strengths, and turn weaknesses into opportunities, and you have done just that for me.

You made me a better person, teaching me that there is richness in humility, opportunity in crisis, and love in anger. The influence you have had on me surpasses that of anyone else; you have shaped me into a more empathetic and sympathetic person. I have learned the art of being quiet, an essential ability for a leader from the beginning. An effective leader is one who can listen, understand, and be solution-oriented. I have learned all this from you, Mr. Nirbhay Vassa, the man who shaped my mind.

You gave me the realisation that the relationship, Harvey and Mike share, is not just a television facade; it can be a reality too.

Sketching Success: Gauri's Portrait of Mentorship

I began my journey at Abans straight out of my internship, like an artist facing a blank canvas, filled with excitement and trepidation. Navigating my first job was daunting, but Nirbhay Sir, our CFO, became the steady brushstrokes shaping my growth, both professionally and personally.

From the start, he encouraged me to take on challenging tasks, his belief in my potential like vibrant splashes of colour boosting my confidence. One key lesson was to focus on my strengths while improving my weaknesses, much like a skilled artist revealing a masterpiece within a block of marble. This made me feel valued and motivated, adding depth to my professional portrait.

When I made mistakes, Nirbhay's exceptional handling turned errors into learning experiences. His constructive feedback and patient mentorship were gentle brushstrokes, refining my skills and helping me become more resilient.

Nirbhay's guidance showed that true leadership is about inspiring others, cultivating responsibility, and leading with integrity. His unwavering support has been a beacon of inspiration, like the guiding light in a painting.

As an artist, I see the world differently, finding beauty in unexpected places. Nirbhay Sir has been like a master painter, guiding me to blend the vibrant colours of my strengths with the softer hues of my weaknesses, creating a balanced image of who I am today.

His influence has made me stronger and more confident, better prepared for career challenges. I aspire to embody his qualities and carry forward his lessons, much like an artist striving to perfect their craft and leave a lasting legacy on their canvas.

In the end, my journey under Nirbhay sir's mentorship has been like the creation of a masterpiece, each stroke of guidance and support adding depth and dimension to my professional self. His influence has been the palette from which I draw strength and inspiration, crafting a career that is as vibrant and meaningful as any piece of art.

Vikas' Reflection: Empowered Leadership

"Nirbhay is the best manager and leader I have had the privilege to work with. When I first joined his team, I was a shy individual with low self-confidence. Nirbhay's mentorship transformed me. He guided me in developing my interpersonal and leadership skills, teaching me how to present myself confidently in front of others. His unwavering trust and confidence in my abilities significantly boosted my self-esteem.

Nirbhay was like a shield, protecting us from the complexities and challenges of our work. This allowed us to perform our duties wholeheartedly, without the constant fear of mistakes and errors. After spending nine long years at my previous job, I took a leadership role at a new organisation, inspired by Nirbhay's example. My aspiration is to emulate his leadership style, creating an environment where people enjoy their work and always feel empowered and protected."

A Journey of Resilience and Triumph: Prachi's Gratitude

I met Mr. Nirbhay Vassa in March 2021 during a challenging time in my CA Finals preparation. On my third attempt, I was starting to doubt myself, but Mr. Vassa's words, "The number of attempts doesn't matter," gave me the confidence to keep going.

I joined Abans as an Associate where Mr. Vassa, the Group CFO, guided us juniors like a peer. His ability to connect and his belief in my potential helped me overcome my fears and grow professionally. Over three years, he ensured everyone felt safe and included, making a lasting impact.

Despite my professional growth, my academic progress stalled. After a discussion with Mr. Vassa, post-November 2023 results, he granted me a three-month study leave, offering the time, motivation, and faith I needed. As a result, I passed my CA exams in July 2024, becoming CA Prachi Uparkar.

I am incredibly fortunate to have had Mr. Vassa as a mentor and friend. His support has been crucial to my professional and personal growth. Being a woman, I never felt neglected or unbiased under his leadership at the workplace.

Thank you, Nirbhay sir, for inspiring me, believing in me, pushing me to become the best version of myself, and for being there for me.

A Tribute to My Mentor: Mahiti's Reflection

Nirbhay Sir, you have been the most significant influence in my life. You have not only guided and supported me but also helped me understand and believe in myself. I feel incredibly fortunate to work alongside you, learning the various aspects of leadership and how to handle tough situations with grace.

From you, I have learned the importance of connecting with peers, valuing everyone around me, and always having empathy towards others. This book is very precious to me and will be to anyone aspiring to be a future leader. Through your experiences, you have beautifully conveyed how a leader should and should not be, and these lessons will undoubtedly help me in my pursuit of becoming a leader like you one day!